AF661888

AVENUES INTO LITERATURE

Avenues into Literature

DR. C.J. O'BRIEN

Commonwealth

Avenues in to Literature

© Reserved

Edition : 2024

ISBN 81-7169-083-1

Published by :

COMMONWEALTH PUBLISHERS
4831/24, Prahlad Street,
Ansari Road, Darya Ganj,
New Delhi - 110002
Ph. : 23275511, 23257835
e-mail : commonwealthbooks@gmail.com

Typesetting by :

Arnav Computers
Delhi

Printed at :
Roshan Offset Printers
New Delhi

DEDICATED
to
My Father
(Late Dr. A.P. O'Brien, Ex-Professor
Banaras Hindu University)

Foreword

I have great pleasure in recommending Dr. C.J. O' Brien's book entitled *Avenues into Literature* which is a collection of various topics on different forms of literature. A youngman from a prominent, though a small state of India, i. e. Orissa, has made a bold attempt to express his ideas in different essays which will be of great help and interest to the young students of literature. Although it is first attempt of Dr. O' Brien in the field of literary criticism in a limited way, it expresses his genuine interest in English literature as well as his intense desire to acquaint the young students with some of the literary topics which aim at giving a critical insight into some of the important problems of English literature.

The book appears to be particularly designed for Indian students, and I hope it will serve some purposes of those students who are really interested in English literature. Dr. O' Brien has expressed some of his views and critical comments and they do deserve serious consideration of all thoughtful Indian students.

I wish allsucc ss to Dr. O' Brien in his bold attempt in getting this published.

Professor and Head of the
Post-Graduate Deptt. of
English Ravenshaw
College-Cuttack.
(M.Q. Khan)

Preface

Literature deals with the values of life. These values are reflected through various forms of Literature—Poetry, Drama, Fiction and Criticism, belonging to different centuries.

> "Each century, as we look back on it, has its own shape and quality, but the seventeenth century overlaps into the eighteenth, the eighteenth into the nineteenth, the nineteenth into the twentieth, the stream is continuous, indivisible, yet each stretch of water has it unique character".[1]

All the articles deal with the varied forms in the garb of various topics of literature.

Finally, I must conclude by thanking my esteemed Professor, Dr. M.Q. Khan of Ravensvaw College, Cuttack, for enlightening me and going through the manuscript.

English Department,

Salipur College, C.J. O'BRIEN
(Utkal University)
ORISSA.

1. *Fifty years of English Literature*, 1900-1950 by R.A. Scott-James, published in 1951, 167, page 1 (Longmans).

Contents

1

Christopher Marlowe : Dr. Faustus

The text of Dr. Faustus raises more problems than that of any other of Marlowe's works. The play scored an immediate success, received many performances between 1594 and 1597, and the title role became a favourite of Edward Alleyn, the most famous of early Elizabethan tragedians, who had created the heroic style of acting in the part of Tamburlaine. The earliest surviving edition, published in 1604 by Thomas Bushell, contains some 1,500 lines and is referred to by editors as the 'A' text (A1). In 1616 John Wright who had meanwhile acquired the copyright published a new version of the play which runs to about 2,100 lines and is now known as the 'B' text or B1. The additional materials relate almost entirely to the scenes in the middle of the play which describe Faustus' achievements at Rome and in Germany. The theory elaborated by W.W. Greg, the most eminent of modern Marlovian editors, is that the 'A' text is an abridged reconstruction, probably made from memory of an earlier text, and that it is the latter which has come down to us as 'B'. Nevertheless from a literary, as distinct from a textual point of view, a number of critics regard 'A' (even when the texts closely resemble one another) as a finer and therefore more characteristically Marlovian work than 'B'. Professor Greg has produced a parallel text edition which prints 'A' and 'B' on opposite pages and provides the most satisfactory method of studying the play. The present study refers to Professor John Jump's edition in the 'Revels plays series' (Methuen). This is mainly based upon 'B', uses modern spelling and follows the example of A1 and B1 in arranging the play as a succession of scenes, instead of imposing an artificial five-act division as Greg and Boas have done. Professor Jump's arrangement of the scenes is grouped as follows :

Scenes 1— 4 correspond to Act I Scenes 1—4
Scenes 5— 7 correspond to Act II Scenes 1—3
Scenes 8—10 correspond to Act III Scenes 1—3
Scenes 11—17 correspond to Act IV Scenes 1—7
Scenes 19—20 correspond to Act V Scenes 1—3

The date of composition of *Dr. Faustus* has been much disputed. At first it was generally believed to have been an early work, written immediately after *Tamburlaine*. Subsequent research has tended to the view that this was Marlowe's last play written in 1592, barely a year before the poet met his death, stabbed in a tavern brawl. This conclusion upon the development of the more flexible type of blank verse in which Faustus' final speeches are written, and partly upon the probability, cogently argued by W.W. Greg, that the play's principal source, an English translation from the German entitled *The History of the Damnable Life of Dr. Faustus*, was not published until 1592. There are important differences of detail between the English and German versions of the story, and it is always the English source which Marlowe follows. It is well worth studying the relationship of *The Damnable Life* to the play, both for the resemblances (the dramatist frequently borrows episodes, ideas and whole phrases), and for the dissimilarities, which often illuminate the originality of Marlow's conception. Other modern scholars, however, such as Kocher, Mahood and Steenan consider that the play shows many more affinities to the heroic dignity of *Tamburlaine* than to the bitter and deflating mood of *The Jew of Malta* and *Edward II* and in the absence of conclusive evidence, support the earlier date of composition.

The authorship of the play presents yet another unsolved problem. The conception is undoubtedly Marlowe's, but the execution is uneven in quality and inconsistent in its details : not only does the writing alternate between sublime poetry and indifferent hack work in verse or prose, but the character of Faustus as displayed in the Wittenberg scenes is quite different from that of the mischievous miracle worker and practical joker at the Vatican or the Imperial Court. In effect the passages which show clear evidence of Marlowe's hand occupy less than half of the play. These are Scenes 1, 3, 5 and the first part of 6 (roughly up to the appearance of the Seven Deadly Sins), the first part of 8 (which describes the approach to Rome), Chorus 1 and 2, the last three scenes and the epilogue. The remainder comprises most of the prose scenes of comic relief, played by Wagner, the scholars and their servants, and the central section of the play (scenes 8-18) which represents Faustus' adventures on his travels. Some of these scenes are in prose, others in a straightforward, sententious and distinctly pedestrian blank verse that lacks the speed, the resonance and the imaginative power which distinguish Marlowe's poetry at its best. The most likely candidate as co-author is generally considered to be Samuel Rowley, an actor and journeyman writer who collaborated with many of the playwrights of his time : a case has also been made out, less convincingly, for the collaboration of Thomas Nashe.

Whatever the nature of the collaboration, the writing of the play presents curious blend of old and new dramatic styles and conventions. The metrical flexibility and imaginative depth of Faustus' speeches in the final scene point forward to the use which Shakespeare was to make of the soliloquy in his great tragedies. On the other hand such devices as the 'pastime' of the Seven Deadly Sins (Scene 6), or the appearance of the Good and Bad Angels, look back to the staging of the medieval morality plays. The characterization also follows the conventions of the medieval rather than of the Elizabethan theatre, with the exception of Faustus and Mephostophilis. The other actors in the drama are personifications of abstract qualities or historical puppets *rather than characters in the Shakespearean sense, while the* blending of crudely farcical interludes with serious speculations on the subject of redemption of damnation is likewise characteristic of the medieval taste for juxtaposing the highest with lowest.

The story of Dr. Faustus, a German scholar who was believed to have sold his soul to the Devil in exchange for the enjoyment of supernatural powers, originated in the early sixteenth century. But the theme of the legend, the human *impulse to seek out forbidden knowledge and transcend the* limits of mortality, is one of the oldest in the mythology of mankind. It occurs especially often in Judaic literature, first of all, of course, in the fable of the Tree of knowledge and the disobedience of Adam and Eve. It reappears with the story of Simon Magus, a sorcerer who tried to purchase from the Apostles the power to confer the gift of the Holy Ghost, who conjured up the spirit of Helen of Troy, and was killed when his attempted flight to Heaven was frustrated by St. Peter. Jewish literature is likewise the source of the idea of a pact made with the Devil to obtain magical powers, as also of the details of the ritual which Faustus employs to summon up the spirits of Hell. And, from another point of veiw, the suspicion that intellectual curiosity is sacrilegious and evil has persisted ever since the triumph of Christianity exalted divine revelation over human science. In the sixteenth century (and indeed later) the distinction between science and magic was by no means clear : to the popular mind the *scientist and the magician resembled each other in* that each had acquired a degree of control over the elements and thus to some extent emancipated himself alike from the Commandments and from the laws of nature.

In any event it was no coincidence that the legend of Dr. Faustus came to birth in Europe when it did. The play echoes the widespread conflict which was taking place at this time between the traditional *faith of Christianity and the* sudden and intoxicating awareness of human capacities *which were becoming evident on every hand* in the discovery of new worlds, new arts, new sciences. It was Marlowe who first perceived the dramatic possibilities of the story which is a natural extension of his first study in human ambition and self-sufficiency, *Tamburlaine.* In this play he explores the desire for a god-like power over the life and death of others. In *Faustus* his theme is the desire for knowledge which in the eyes of his protagonist (again, like Tamburlaine, a humbly born self-made hero) far exceeds the authority of the ruler.

> All things that move between quiet poles,
> Shall be at my command : Emperors and Kings
> Are but obeyed in their several provinces.
> But his dominion that exceeds in this
> Stretches as far as doth the mind of man (I. 55-59)

and in this quest Faustus is remorselessly spurred on by the typically Marlovian sentiment that 'peril is the chiefest way to happiness'.

At the same time this powerful impulse towards self-reliance is offset by a crushing sense of fatalism. The celebrated Renaissance boast 'Men can do all things if they will' is followed by total disillusionment when humanity discovers its limitations. It is between these extremes of exultation and despair that the action of Dr. Faustus is plotted. A sentence from *The Damnable Life* indicates the spiritual trap in which the hero is caught.

> Dr. Faustus was even pondering with himself how he might get loose from so damnable an end as he had given himself, both of body and soul : but his repentance was like to that of Cain and Judas, he thought his sins greater than God could forgive, and here upon rested his mind.

In this context it becomes necessary to remember the difference between the modern attitude to this theme and that of Marlowe and his contemporaries. The modern reader, influenced no doubt by Goethe's and other authors' treatment of the subject, is perhaps primarily moved by curiosity : he is interested in the hero's psychology, he wishes to know what gratification of the intellect, spirit or senses Faustus received from his twenty-four years of supernatural power. Marlowe's interest, by contrast, is primarily religious : he is concerned with Faustus' gradual estrangement from his salvation. In other words, the tragedy hinges upon Faustus' inability to repent (which is caused by his despair), and it is to this theme that the playwright again and again returns.

Dr. Faustus' opening soliloquy shows him at the returning point of his career. He has mastered the philosophy, the learned professions, the experimental sciences of his day but, as he ponders the nature and purpose of his studies, he rejects every one in turn. He chafes against the accepted limits of intellectual and spiritual discipline. 'Settle thy studies', begin : these terms suggest an impatient desire to embrace a new and radical choice which will change the whole purpose and direction of his mental processes—in a word : 'begin to live'. He finds no ideal of service in the practice of medicine, or of justice in the study of the law. These professions seem to him mere drudgery, because no amount of proficiency in them can exempt him from the unwelcome reminder

Yet art thou still but Faustus and a man

Lastly he turns to divinity, not in a spirit of humility but rather as the subject most worthy of his intellectual powers. But this too he dismisses by a deliberate distortion of the text of the Bible. The first quotation : 'The reward of sin is death', taken from St. Paul's Epistle to the Romans, VI, 23, should be followed by the words, 'but the gift of God is eternal life', and the second, 'If we say that we have no sin, we deceive ourselves' (1st Epistle of St. John, I, 8) by the words, 'If we confess our sins, he is faithful and just to forgive us our sins'. These texts on the subject of redemption would have been known by heart to many of Marlowe's audience, who could not have failed to notice the sophistry of their omission. By suppressing them, Faustus takes the first of his wilful steps away from his salvation.

The appearances of the good and bad angels at this point, and at later intervals in the play, mark the various phases in Faustus' temptation. He succumbs at once to the lure of wealth and power, and when at the end of Scene 1 he joins forces with two German magicians, Valdes and Cornelius, he has already chosen a course of intellectual degradation which will frustrate the very search for knowledge for which he is ready to barter his soul.

In Scene 3 Faustus pursues temptation a step further and succeeds in conjuring up the Devil Mephostophilis. This brings together the two personages whose interaction dominates the entire play. Man is directly confronted with the representative of evil (whom he has summoned on his own initiative) and Marlowe draws a sharp contrast between the characteristics of the two. Faustus is arrogant and overconfident in his newly-found skill in magic. He imagines Mephostophilis to be his personal attendant, 'full of obediences and humility'. Mephostophilis makes it clear first that he owes no obedience to Faustus:

I am a servant to great Lucifer

And may not follow thee without his leave and secondly that he has come not because of the power of Faustus' spells, but because he seems a promising candidate for damnation. Faustus on the other hand remains oblivious of his peril, boasts that he has no fear of hell and urges Mephostophilis to learn manly fortitude. His egotism blinds him to Mephostophilis' suffering, which consists not of the crude torments of traditional hell-fire, but of the anguish of the soul which is severed from God.

Why this is hell, nor am I out of it. Mephostophilis on the other hand is quite unlike the satanic tampter presented by Goethe or Gounod. He does not attempt to lure his victim: it is Faustus who arrogantly despatches him with the offer of his soul:

Go bear these tidings to great Lucifer

More than any other Elizabethan play, *Dr. Faustus* relies upon the soliloquy. Much of Faustus' own role consists of solitary meditation, and many of the lines which, technically speaking, are delivered by other characters, could be regarded as the voice of conscience or temptation. The opening of the fifth scene marks the next stage on Faustus' downward path. He has now fallen into despair, a state of mind in which the victim rejects consolation and prevents himself from seeking deliverance. Faustus has turned his will and his understanding upside down. The trust and resolve of which he is still capable are to be diverted from God and devoted to the Devil:

When Mephostophilis shall stand by me

What power can hurt me? Faustus, thou art safe. The 'glad tidings' which he impatiently awaits from Lucifer turn out to be the demand that he shall write a testament to sign away his soul. This he does, in spite of the warning he receives when his blood refuses to flow and the words '*Home, fuge*' (Fly O man!) appears on his arm. He seals the bargain with the blasphemous quotation '*Consummatum est*', the last words of Christ on the Cross.

The pact completed, Faustus is free to pursue his quest for knowledge and for pleasure. His first request again betrays the superficiality which is his besetting weakness. Because he is wanton and lascivious, he asks for a wife. But this demand, since marriage is a sacrament, Mephostophilis cannot fulfil and he is obliged to explain that what Faustus really wants is a mistress.

At the beginning of the sixth scene Faustus experiences yet another crisis of conscience and is torn between a lingering desire to repent and his terror of the consequences if he does so. Here with the lines:

Have I not made blind Homer sing to me
Of Ariadne's love and Oenon's death?
And hath not he, that built the walls of Thebes
With ravishing sound of his melodious harp
Made music with my Mephostophilis?

Why should I die then or basely despair? (VI 26-31)
Marlowe touches upon another important facet of his hero's

character, which he shares with Tamburlaine, a love of beauty, a power of imagination and an ability to express it in words, qualities which in Faustus' case produce a fatal tendency to invest sin with heroic illusions. Faustus as it were hypnotizes himself and succumbs to temptations which he, not Mephostophilis, has conjured up.

In the dialogue which follows concerning astrology and meteorology (VI 35-75) Faustus has not extended his knowledge far before he is abruptly halted in his enquiry

Now tell me who made the world? to which Mephostophilis refuses point blank to reply, since devils are prohibited from naming God. This provokes a final rebellion from Faustus, so serious that, for once, the Good Angel is allowed the last word, and Faustus' prayer:

> Ah Christ my Saviour, my Saviour
> Help to save distressed Faustus' soul

produces the immediate entry of Lucifer. This is in a sense the point of no return in the play, the last occasion on which Faustus might have summoned the strength to redeem himself. As it is he is paralysed by the horror of Lucifer's appearance and at once promises to renounce his salvation.

In the central section of the play, (Scenes 7-17) the tension is noticeably relaxed. The battle for Faustus' soul has been fought : what follows is a diversion in which he enjoys his (largely illusory) gains. Marlowe's hand is only occasionally traceable, and in general these episodes may be regarded as following a scenario which he may have outlined, but allowed to be executed for the most part by others. The impression created by the two central characters undergoes a decided change. Mephostophilis has become the genial, worldly wise boon companion, while Faustus oscillates between youthful high spirits, love of mischief, and occasional premonitions of his approaching doom.

With Scene 18 and the opening of the fifth act the vanities of Faustus' miracle-working grand tour are behind us, and Marlowe's mature style re-appears as the play moves towards its climax. The Old Man, whose humility and compassion are contrasted with Faustus' intellectual pride and wilfulness makes a last appeal not to let sin by custom grow into nature. Again Faustus is tormented by his incapacity for repentance.

> Hell strives with grace for conquest in my breast

but at the first threat from Mephostophilis his resistance coapses. He calls down torments upon the Old Man, and to seal his surrender asks for Helen of Troy as his paramour and launches into the famous apostrophe

> Was this the face that launched a thousand ships
> And burned the topless towere of Ilium?

This speech has become so famous as an anthology piece, a rhapsody upon a vision of supreme beauty, that it is easy to lose sight of its context in the play. Faustus has asked for Helen to extinguish his thoughts of Heaven. She is not a woman of flesh and blood, but an apparition whose beauty is but skin-deep, indeed worse, an evil spirit, as becomes clear from the fourth line

> Her lips suck forth my soul, see where it flies and the deliberate blasphemy of

> *Here* will I dwell, for heaven is in *these* lips. At the same time the images of idealized beauty are strikingly blended with metaphors of destruction. For Helen's sake Ilium is burned and Wittendurg sacked; her splendour is compared to the lightning of Jupiter which reduced Semele to ashes and to the white heat which purges precious metals; '(all is dross that is not Helena)'—this last metaphor harking back to Mephostophilis' reference to the Day of Judgement

> When all the world dissolves
> And every creature shall be purified (V. 125-26)

It is significant that after the seventh line (all is dross) the Old Man re-enters to hear the remainder of the speech and instantly recognises—despite its grandeur and its suggestion of the world well lost for love—the final refusal of grace which Faustus' words imply.

After the superb rhetoric of this speech—the last that Marlowe wrote in the Tamburlaine manner—the contrasting quiet of the next scene in which Faustus bids farewell to his fellow-scholars is all the more dramatically powerful: it is one of the rare occasions when Marlowe resorts to prose. Faustus has given himself up 'for lost', 'too late' is the burden of the whole scene, and 'the date is expired' he tells his friends. At the same time he is still capable of affection for others and we may wonder how a man whose heart has been hardened beyond repentance should at the last feel so much solicitude for his friends : 'Talk not of me, but save yourselves and depart'. In this last act Faustus' suffering achieves the dimensions of tragedy precisely because we feel that he has recovered something of his moral sense, has been brought face to face with the real nature of his choice and has begun to understand it.

Time is the dominating theme of the final soliloquy (19.134) which is ushered in by the striking of the clock. The last hour of Faustus' life is dramatically compressed into a bare sixty lines and the true significance of time past and time to come flashes upon him, as if before the eyes of a drowning man. The life that has been given him is at its last gasp : the damnation he has called down upon himself is everlasting. The movement of the verse is superbly fitted to its purpose :

> Now hast thou but one bare hour to live
> And then thou must be damned perpetually

a sequence of slow heavy monosyllables reaching their climax in 'perpetually', the word which epitomises Faustus' terror, progressing to the frantic irregularity of

> One drop would save my soul, half a drop.
> Ah, my Christ !

as Marlowe—yet again—seems to hold salvation just out of Faustus' reach. At the end of the scene the circle is complete. Faustus, whose pride had tempted him to raise himself above mortal stature, begs to be allowed to renounce his humanity, to become a brutish beast, or better still to be annihilated utterly.

O Soul, be chang'd into little water drops
And fall into the ocean, ne'er be found. (19.185-6)

Critics and commentators have continued to debate whether Marlowe's sympathies lie with Faustus, or whether, himself a notorious free-thinker, he wrote the play as a vindication of the orthodox Christian viewpoint. Neither hypothesis is entirely convincing. Marlowe is remorseless in his condemnation of his hero : the thief upon the Cross, even the serpent that tempted Eve may be saved, but not Faustus. In the words of one of his acutest critics, Harry Levin, Marlowe achieves the conviction of sin without the belief in salvation. It is precisely the fact that Faustus is capable of apprehending Heaven but not of attaining it that gives his story its tragic quality; for tragedy is not mitigated by faith, but makes its effect by its uncompromising confrontation of the worst that life can do to man.

2

The Soliloquies of Hamlet

The soliloquy is an age old dramatic convention. A character thinks aloud in his soliloquy and thereby reveals himself and his inner conflict and his motive. The soliloquies in *Hamlet* enrich the spiritual and poetic quality of the play. Without the soliloquies Hamlet with its *Senecan* melodramatic materials of unnatural deeds, incest, insanity, murders and deaths would be little better than Kyd's *The Spanish Tragedy*. In fact Shakespeare transforms melodrama into tragedy in his play and the soliloquies help in this regard. They make Hamlet a most moving character, a soul seen in a spiritual crisis.

There are seven soliloquies in Hamlet, *two* in Act I, *one* in Act II, *three* in Act III and *one* in Act IV. The first soliloquy begins

"O, that this too too solid flesh would melt,
Thaw and resolve itself into a deer!"

Hamlet wants to commit suicide. Mr. Robertson says that the play deals with the effect of a mother's guilt upon her son. This thought of suicide is in excess of the fact. There is no objective correlative, as Eliot writes in his essay on *Hamlet* (1919). Hamlet expresses emotion but cannot connect it with 'a set of objects, a chain of events, which shall be the formula of that particular emotion'. In fact in the soliloquies there is this lack of an objective correlative to precisely define the emotion. The first soliloquy ends with the generalization "Frailty thy name is woman" which shows another point of Hamlet, how he passes from himself to humanity as Barbara Burge writes in 'The Identity of Hamlet' published in *The Review of English Literature* (1964).

The second soliloquy, also, in Act I, is after the departure of the ghost. He follows the injunction of the ghost "Hamlet! remember me" with the words "Remember thee!" repeated twice. He will now wipe away all "from the table of his memory". He speaks of his mother as "pernicious woman" and of Claudius "that one may smile and smile, and be a villain". Hamlet in the soliloquy resolves to take revenge on his uncle. The ghost is taken, as Dover Wilson writes in his book *Elizabethen Spiritualism*, as reality and revenge as it was then regarded as a religious duty.

In the third soliloquy in Act 2, Sc. 2, Hamlet accuses himself: "Now I am alone/O what a rogue and peasant slave am I". He doubts the ghost: "The spirit I have seen may be the devil". He wants evidence: "the play's the thing wherein I'll catch the conscience of the thing".

Here we are centered in the delay in action in Hamlet. He hesitates, doubts, procastinates, a feature progressing throughout the play. In the soliloquy we find argument and shifts of feeling.

The fourth soliloquy in Act 3, Sc. 1, the "To be or not to be" soliloquy is the most artistic and revealing. He considers human life, 'the mind to suffer', death and after life. He reverts to himself "a bare bodkin" would end all. From philosophic considerations of life and death for man, he speaks of the eternal, "The undiscovered country from whose bourn/No traveller returns". He speaks of conscience and his inaction "sicklied over with the pale cast of thought". Finally he remembers Ophelia idealized "Nymph in thy Orisons". He remembers his father's death and of Death as a whole of which it is a symbol. Hamlet]is, as Wilson Knight writes in *The Wheel of Fire*, "the ambassador of Death walking amidst life".

The fifth soliloquy in Act 3, Sc. 2 is a relatively short one. It shows the progress of the action. He can "drink hot blood" but he will rouse the conscience of his mother "I will speak daggers to her". This leads to the Bedroom scene. The sixth soliloquy in Act 3, Sc. 3 is also a short one. He finds Claudius kneeling and says "Now might I do it pat". But he will not as Claudius will then go to heaven and Hamlet's revenge encompasses both his body and soul. Both these soliloquies account for delay in action.

In the seventh and last soliloquy in Act 4, Sc.4 he speaks of his "dull revenge" and of his "thinking too precisely on the event". He resolves:

> "O from this time forth
> My thoughts be bloody."

Four Acts have passed and Hamlet has done nothing except theoretically to kill the King in the death of Polonius.

All these soliloquies lead to an analysis of Hamlet's character to explain delay. Goethe finds him sensitive, Coleridge an intellectual, and Bradley as morally sensitive, all of which retard action. The fact remains that Hamlet is a play of inaction. It is an introspective tragedy. This accounts for his constant argument, explication and questioning in the soliloquies. The soliloquies are essential to a study of the character of Hamlet. But the soliloquies are a *part* of the play which is a complex of many issues, delay, madness and the antic disposition, comic scenes like Grave-digger's scene to relieve the gloom of the play, Doubt, Interrogation and Irony which Harry Levin brings out in *The Question of Hamlet* (1959).

3

William Shakespeare : Julius Caesar

Julius Caesar marks an interesting stage in the evolution of Shakespeare's style. In no other play, perhaps, does he show such a relaxed command of the blank verse form, originally inherited from Marlowe and now considerably refined and sophisticated in the course of writing some fifteen plays, that is, about half of his work. The verse runs smoothly in the pentameter form, without any sense of forcing: ideas and imagery remain well within the dramatist's control. There is no grasping after the inexpressible, or bursting through the limitations of syntax and usage such as characterize the most powerful passages of the later work. In *Julius Caesar* we have the style of limited perfection, as Bradley observed: fluent, lucid and flexible, responding easily to a wide range of rhetorical and dramatic demands.

Sir Thomas North published his version of Plutarch's *Lives of the Noble Grecians and Romans* in 1579. This collection of historical biographies, widely read in Elizabethan England, provided the raw material from which Shakespeare constructed his Roman plays, in this instance from the lives of Caesar, Brutus and Antony. The Penguin *Shakespeare's Plutarch*, or the extracts in the appendix to the Arden edition of the play, render this source material easily available to the student, who might well begin by comparing the original material for the Formu scene with what Shakespeare eventually makes of it, as a measure of the dramatist's creative genius. In some parts, the debt to Plutarch is much greater, and occasionally even extends to phrasing. Because he had recently completed his study of a successful general and politician in the name-part in *Henry V*, Shakespeare may well have welcomed the chance to make Brutus, rather than Caesar, the protagonist of his first Roman tragedy. The idea of a man of thoughtful disposition and good intentions caught up in a current of violent political action clearly interested Shakespeare, who had begun to explore the theme in *Henry VI* and (minus the good intentions) *Richad II*, and was, of course, to crown his study of it in *Hamlet*. As he read through the life of Brutus in North's book, he must have seen at once that here was a situation not only interesting as a study in human nature, but wonderfully suited to dramatization, both in terms of conflict within the mind of the 'hero', and of the external conflicts naturally surrounding a political assassination. I use the term 'here' because, whatever the title may appear to say on the subject, the play is more rightly understood as the tragedy of Brutus than of Caesar. The criteria of Shakespearian tragedy synthesized by Bradley are entirely applicable: a man with enormous potential for good brought to an evil and through some weakness in his own temperament, coupled with the implication of man's nobility and worth even when thus driven to self-destruction. Furthermore, it is largely in Bradley's terms of character issuing in action that this play may most profitably be studied.

A general word of caution, however. This is a political play, and it is therefore appropriately constructed in terms of propaganda and subjective comment, which we must beware of taking at its face value. Cassius' passionate condemnation of Caesar in the second scene, for instance, where the speaker is pressing all his rhetorical art into service to win Brutus over to his cause, yields negligible motives for assassination when the passion is filtered off and the residue subjected to logical analysis—as Cassius goes more than half way towards confessing, in his short soliloquy after Brutus' exit. The reader must constantly consider the motives behind each speech, as well as the surface meaning. With this proviso in mind, let us consider some of the major actors in this political drama.

Widely differing accounts of Shakespeare's Caesar have been given. It is possible, by selecting only details that fit the case and ignoring other evidence, to show the Caesar of this play as physically decrepit, superstitious, vacillating, vain and bombastic; in other words, a Caesar in decline. However, an overall consideration of his actions in the play reveals a magnanimous leader whose authority rests on competence, but is human enough to share some of the common failings of mankind. The opening speeches of Flavius and Marullus are, of course, loaded against him, as these two are strong adherents of the recently defeated Pompey. Caesar has little chance, in his short first appearance in procession, of establishing a very positive image of himself, although Shakespeare is at pains to make clear his absolute authority in Antony's words: 'When Caesar says "Do this," it is performed', and in the instant response of the procession to Caesar's wishes. After Caesar has moved off, it is Cassius' turn to paint a picture of him in a series of passionate tirades, as brilliant in their way as anything that Shakespeare has written. Stripped of their passion and rhetoric, however, what remains? That Cassius was a better swimmer than Caesar, and that once when Caesar was lying fever-stricken, he felt thirsty. We really learn more of the true nature of Cassius than of Caesar from this invective, and he comes very near to an explicit admission of his jealousy in the speech beginning, 'Why, man, he doth bestride the narrow world....' Indeed, Brutus' failure to penetrate to the hollow core of this argument is a severe comment on his powers of reasoning, and Cassius in his final soliloquy declares that he would not have been moved by such argument if the situations were reversed.

Meanwhile Caesar returns from the games, and in ten lines or so to Antony tells us more truth about Cassius than the latter gave us about Caesar in nearly a hundred. It is a penetrating analysis, worth careful study, not less because it rounds off with a characteristic touch of vanity:

I always tell thee what is to be feared
Than what I fear, for always I am Caesar.

At the same time, we must recognize that Caesar's belief in his courage is nowhere at variance with his conduct. Again, however, he is only given the barest chance to establish himself before the procession passes on, and it is now Casca's turn to paint him in an unfavourable, even ludicrous, light which, by means of his blunt and highly subjective account, he does superbly enough. We should not be deceived by this tart humour into thinking other than that a man suffering from epilepsy had one of his accustomed bouts at a very awkward moment, from which he recovered to make a public apology which was well received.

Up to this point I have considered Shakespeare's presentation of Caesar in some detail in order to demonstrate the discriminatory technique required to form a fair estimate, but I must now pass on to his final appearance in the Senate, where a different question is at issue. The charge here is that of an extreme arrogance, almost amounting to megalomania. His last two speeches certainly show that he had a very high opinion of his own determination and are couched in grandiloquent, if poetically very effective, terms:

But I am constant as star...

and so forth. Here I think a different sort of allowance must be made, arising from two factors. The first is a dramatic one: Shakespeare had to combine suspense with the arousal of a certain sympathy for the conspirators, if the full emotional possibilities of the situation were to be realized. Secondly, a dislike for flattery is in keeping with Caesar's character (I place little weight on Decius' cheap sneer) and Shakespeare certainly makes Metellus Cimber, in his florid address and prostrated attitude, go out of his way to earn the rebuke that he receives in such heavy measure.

So Caesar dies, but not his influence, which remains dominant until the end of the play. Even while the assassins stand round him with their weapons thick with Caesar's blood, Antony cannot forbear reminding them of his former triumphs, and he late apostrophizes the corpse as 'the ruins of the noblest man that ever lived…'. His prophecy that Caesar's spirit shall return from Hados to inflict a bitter revenge is entirely true of the remainder of the action, for it can be argued that Caesar dead, dramatically speaking, has a greater influence than Caesar living. His name is constantly invoked during the rest of the play; even Brutus and Cassius in their private bickering, for instance, find occasion to make appeal to his memory three times, Brutus' first words on learning of Cass' death are:

> O Julius Caesar, thou art mighty yet!
> Thy spirit walks abroad…

and he himself dies with Caesar's name upon his lips.

Brutus wins our admiration by the unquestioned sincerity of his regard for honour and the welfare of the Roman state. Even the cynical Casca does not imply that his reputation among the Romans is anything but deserved: 'O, he sits high in all the people's hearts…'. He is an idealist, unsuited to the world of *realpolitik*: once he assumed direction of the conspirators his idealism ceased to be a source of strength and became a disability, leading him to make two disastrous decisions: first, allowing Antony to live, and second, letting him speak at the funeral. Idealism, however, was not the quality that led to his downfall, but rather a failure to reason clearly, and to see that he was being manipulated by others to serve their own private ends. In the important soliloquy 'It must be by his death . . .' no adequate reason is given for killing Caesar, the whole basis of the argument is hypothetical. The speech is eloquent, perhaps at first sight plausible, but it cannot bear analysis: it is as if Brutus' own powers of reasoning were blinded for the moment by his clever use of imagery and rhetoric. He even admits that he has never known Caesar's emotions to get the better of his reason, in the light of which his conclusion, 'Then lest he *may*, prevent . . .' is pitifully inadequate. It is not disputed that he *thinks* he is choosing the more honourable alternative in killing his friend: the tragic error is that he should make the wrong choice. Nor is he always even consistent in the high moral attitude that he adopts; in the quarrel scene, for instance, he chides Cassius for raising money by corrupt methods, and in the next breath upbraids him for not sending him funds to pay his soldiers, because he, Brutus, cannot bring himself to raise the money:

> By heaven, I had rather coin my heart,
> And drop my blood for drachmas, than to wring
> From the hard hands of peasants their vile trash
> By any indirection.

Later, he makes some moving observations about the cowardice of suicide, and then tells Cassius that he has determined to kill himself rather than face capture and disgrace. A certain complacency in his rectitude apparently blinds him to the bitter irony of his own last words,

> My heart doth joy that yet, in all my life,
> I found no man but he was true to me . . .

a complacency which may be observed earlier in his taking for granted that he knows best ('Good reasons must of force give way to better . . .'), and which becomes irritatingly obtrusive in the attitude he adopts towards Cassius in the quarrel scene.

Considered in the mass in this way, these shortcomings might seem to discount the feeling of pity for Brutus which is essential if the emotions proper to tragedy are to be generated but in the context of the play they are continually mitigated by our sympathy for the dilemma of divided loyalty, regard for his motives, admiration for his kindly solicitude in his relations with Portia and the boy Lucius, and commiseration towards the end of the play when he has to bear the loss of his wife among so many other blows of fortune. Shakespeare leaves us in no doubt as to where he wishes Brutus to stand in our final estimation when, taking a hint from Plutarch, he gives Antony his final lines:

> This was the noblest Roman of them all;
> All the conspirators save only he
> Did that they did in envy of great Caesar;

He only, in a general honest thought
And common good to all, made one of them.
His life was gentle, and the elements
So mixed in him that Nature might stand up
And say to all the world, 'This was a man!'

Until Caesar's death, Antony is deliberately held in the background. The few lines he speaks give nothing away, but Shakespeare is careful to distribute hints in the mouths of others as to what kind of man this is, for he is hoping to create a powerful effect when Antony is launched into the action of the drama, and anticipation is a useful weapon.

Shakespeare's mastery of the dramatic craft is nowhere better illustrated than in the consummate skill with which Antony is introduced as a figure to be reckoned with in the power contest, from the point of his arrival among the conspirators to the end of the Formu scene. Ignoring the sequence of events in Plutarch, he brings the introduction forward to create a second major wave of tension after the excitement of the murder, and he increases the suspense by preceding Antony's entry with the arrival of his messenger, whose words in some measure outline the nature of the dramatic situation: if Antony is to live how is he to reconcile his love of Caesar with friendship for his murderers? He has, however, one strong card in addition to his own native-wit: Brutus has sent assurance of safe conduct. This allows Antony, immediately on his appearance, to establish his sincerity towards the conspirators by an outburst of implied protest at what they have done, even offering himself as a second sacrifice upon their swords. This is a calculated risk, as the cannot be certain that Brutus, in such a crisis, is in a position to enforce his promise, and he softens the request with a subtle appeal to their self-esteem in the last line: '. . . by you cut off, The choice and master spirits of the age'. The bluff works, and Brutus characteristically offers to appease Antony with reason, and Cassius with an offer of a place in the cabinet. The complex three-cornered relationship between the principals is brilliantly presented, adding its own tensions to those already implicit in the situation. Antony, having established that the conspirators are willing to accept him, has now to win consent to the request that will eventually lead to their downfall. He cleverly makes this point almost as an afterthought, something so much to be taken for granted that no reasonable person could refuse:

> That's all I seek;
> And am moreover suitor that I may
> Produce his body to the market-place
> And in the pulpit, as becomes a friend,
> Speak in the order of his funeral.

Never can those simple words 'and am moreover' have been used to carry greater weight. The opportunist in Antony has saved him for the moment: it now remains to see what he can make of his chance. He is also, however, a warm-hearted human figure, as Shakespeare allows us to see in his soliloquy over Caesar's body when the conspirators have withdrawn. These two qualities, added to a powerful command of rhetoric, will presently enable him to get his way with the crowd. First, however, there is Brutus' speech, which gives an excellent illustration of Shakespeare's ability to suit the manner to the man. It is in prose, the language of reason, and reason is, as we have seen, everthing to Brutus. Here again the reasoning is unimpressive, objectively considered, but it is good enough for the crowd, and working rapidly through tersely-worded antitheses and climaxes to a series of unanswerable rhetorical questions, gains the required effect. It is typical of Brutus to consider that is the end of the matter: his line 'Then none have I offended' has the conclusive certainty of a geometrical theorem: I have given them reasons; they have accepted these reasons; there is no more to be said; and he is sufficiently confident to depart and leave the stage to Antony, a mistake that one cannot imagine Cassius making. Antony begins slowly; after all, he does not know whether he can sway the crowd against the conspirators or not and, if he cannot, then he had better not say anything to make his position in post-Caesarian Rome any more desperate than it is. His chief weapons are irony, logic and appeal to emotion, always supported by a sure feeling for rhetoric form. The logic is reasonable as far as it goes, but it is in reality nothing more than a polished demonstration of argument from selected instances. The two-sided weapon of irony enables him to feel his way without committing himself: there is nothing in his long first speech that he will have to retract if his audience remains loyal to Brutus. Indeed, with a skill in manipulation that outshines even that of Cassius, he is able to play on the emotions of the crowd for a further seventy lines or so, without actually involving himself in accusations against the conspirators. Up to line 165, 'Room for Antony; most noble Antony!' he could still withdraw if it seemed tactically expedient. But as he steps down preparatory to making play with Caesar's mentle, he knows that he is not going to withdraw: he senses strongly that the mood of the crowd is now ready for anything that he will give them, and he has a master-stroke in hand. Lifting a corner of the mentle, he moves insidiously past the implications of such terms as 'envious' Casca, 'cursed' steel, 'ingratitude more strong than traitors' arms' to an inspired climax in which he tears off the robe to reveal the mutilated body, and in the shock of silence which follows, pours out his message with all the power he can command: '. . . marred, as you see, with traitors'. There is no going back from this.

Space forbids consideration of how much of Antony's rhetoric derives from calculation and how much from genuine emotion for his friend: clearly there are strong elements of both, and the two flowing in the same direction give enormous power to Antony's persuasion. His words to himself as the citizens stream off in a mutinous mob should not be overlooked and at the beginning of the next act we gain a further insight into his nature as he coldly trades his nephew's life against that of Lepidus' brother, and later confesses to Octavius his cynical proposal to get what he can out of Lepidus and then discard him. Here is the naked heart of revolutionary politics crystallized for all time. Can we draw any conclusion about Shakespeare's own attitude to politics from the fact that not one of the characters in this play who are drawn into the political arena amerges from the experience unsullied?

4

The Art of Francis Bacon : A Study

Before Bacon there was rich and sonorous prose. Jeremy Taylor wrote *Holy Living* and *Holy Dying*. Hooker a great stylist, wrote *Ecclesiastical Polity* in 1597, the same year Bacon's earliest essays. The sentences are long and full of the "solid slendour" of majestic periods. Seventeen years later Raleigh wrote his famous *History of the World* which contains his memorable apostrophe to Death in the rich complexities of Elizabethan England and its English as found in Hooker and Nash, Deloney and Dekker. Bacon in his writings took a step forward from Elizabethan English. Rhetoric to him was a deceitful art. He gives his theory of the function of language. He wrote the "first distemper of learning, when men study words and not matter" for "words are but the images of matter". He believed in"the referential function" of language for exact description and rational analysis which his essays demonstrate. He regarded the "expressive function" of language as subordinate. His manner was to express 'assertive will and practical reasons at the expense generally of the more delicately perceptive elements of the sensibility' as L.C. Knights states in *Explorations* (1946). Bacon was the founder of modern scinentific rationalism.

Dr. Rudolf Metz writes that 'The Pragmatic Utilitarianism of the Bacon Philosophy' for practical ends made him shift from art to "technics" of language. He sought clear expression rather than "fineness and affectation of phrases" as Dr. Rawley, Bacan's chaplain and literary executor comments.

Bacon's *Essays or Counsels, Civil and Morals* appeared in three editions, the 1597 edition entitled *Ten Essays*, the 1612 edition, under the caption *Essays* and the 1625 edition. The Essays in Style and Matter can be divided into categories, the early essays of 1597 and the latter essays of 1612 and 1625 editions. In the Prefatory letter to the Second edition he called The essays "certain brief notes which I called Essays". The term means a trial or tentative effort, or assay, borrowed from Montaigne. Montaigne's essay written fourteen years before Bacon, were informal, self-revealing and discursive; Bacon's are of a *different style, impersonal, brief and descriptive*. Bacon called his essays "dispersed meditations". They were so on diverse subject books, studies and the nature of man. He took the form of the essay from Montaigne but filled it, as Hugh Walker writes in *The English Essay and Essayists*, 'with material drawn from his own mind'. His essays are pithy, full of meaning and thought. He uses techniques of language of his own. In *Of Studies* he writes short and crisp sentences. Each sentence stands by itself and is a concentrated summation of ideas, such as "Studies serve for delight, for ornament, and for ability" or "Reading maketh a full man; conference a ready man; and writing and exact man". He uses aphorisms compact with thought and practical wisdom and garnered experience. In the essay *Of Death*, for example, he writes with rare perception. Revenge Triumps over death; Love slights it; Honour aspireth to it". Each little division in this sentence is independent of the other semantically and structurally. He uses Antithesis. At times he uses a series of antitheses He pairs them off, as in "Histories make men wise, poets witty; the mathematics subtle; natural philosophy, deep, moral grave.' To get at the meaning, the reader has to pause in order to fill out the hiatuses or gaps of thought at the end of the semi-colon. *Another favourite device of Bacon is the use of* analogy to bring out the meaning in *Of Marriage and Single Life* he writes; "A single life doth well with churchmen; for charity will hardly water the ground where it must first fill a pool". To illustrate this point of view Bacon at times gives even homely examples as in *Of Adversity*: "We see in needle works and embroidery: it is now more pleasing to have a lively work upon a sad and solemn ground, than to have a dark and melancholy work upon a lightsome ground."

In Bacon the analogues have value for the support they offer to his thinking.

Bacon had an encyclopaedic mind. His knowledge and his range of regarding were extensive. His essays are full of Allusions which he weaves into the texture of his writing. He refers in *Of Truth,* to Lucian one of the later schools of the Grecians, who wrote that men love lies as poets do after Plato's ideas in the *Republic*. In *Of Parents and Children* he closes the essay with a sentence of Pythagoras to transmit a precept." Choose what is best, custom will make it agreeable and easy". Biblical allusions and quotations in *Of Truth,* the last line has a text from Luke 28 "When Christ cometh, he shall not find falyh upon the earth". In *Of Unity in Religion* he refers to Isiah 14 where the devil said "I will ascend and be like the highest". Geoffery Tillotson in *Essays and Criticism and Research* Chapter 4, "Words for Princes" shows how Bacon wrote for Princes. He wrote of royal gardens and palaces. In *Of Empire* he describes:

> "Princes are like to heavenly bodies, which cause good or evil times". A measure of his writing is in support of King and state. He condemned "Execruble actions of murdering Princes" and the "subversion of states and governments" in *Of Unity in Religion*. Yet Bacon wrote for all men as he mentioned in the second edition (1612): his essays are indeed a "new work" and come home to men business and bosoms". He varies his vocabulary to suit the level of his address.

The Baconian essay particularly of 1597 consisted of a incipient paragraph related to a subject. His method was to weigh and balance matters. The memoranda which they contain are written in an abrupt runic style as exemplified in his essays on Studies, Discurse, Suitors, Expense, Faction, and Negotiating. The essays have few connectives, each sentence standing by itself. Their prose style is an index of the mind of Bacon, the thinker and vigour of his mind for making sharp intellectual formulations.

The later essays reveal Bacon's fine magniloguence. In *Of Truth* he writes with literary power and striking Elizabethan glammer in the jewels he refers to:

> "Truth may perhaps come to the price of a pearl, that sheweth best by day; but it will not rise to the price of a diamond or carbuncle that sheweth best in varied lights".

In *Of Gardens* he writes of the beauty of Nature in different seasons:

> "For March, there come violets, specially the single blue, which are the earliest; The yellow daffodil"; the daisy, the almond tree in blossom; the peech tree in blossom; sweet briar...In July come gilliflowers of all varieties; musk roses; the lime tree in blossom".

The catalogue of beauty are like the description of the pastoral beauty given greater elaboration in Shakespeare's *A Winter's Tale.* Bacon at times has utterance like a poet. In *Of Adversity* he writes: "Virtue is like precious odours, most fragrant when they are incensed or crushed". Like Pope who revealed beauty in his *Satires* Bacon writes of the negative emotion *Of Envy*: "envy is as the sunbeams that beat upon a bank or steep rising ground, than upon a flat. This selective bank image reminds of the splendid bank images which adorn Shakespeare's plays like in *A Mid Summer Night's Dream.* The later essays have a richer virtue than the earlier ones. The imagery as Geoffery Tillotson states "testify to the quality of his subsidiary experience". The Renaissance apears revealingly not only in Bacon's thinking but in the *rhythm* of his sentences as in this example: "Yet even in the Old

Testament, if you listen to Divid's harp, you shall hear as many hearse-like airs or carols; and the pencil of the Holy Ghost hath laboured more in describing the afflictions of Job than the felicities of Solomon" (*Of Adversity*).

Bacon had a variety of styles. In fact "he was a master of numerous and varied styles" as Max Patrick writes in The British Council *Writers and their Works* (1961). He could be sharp, crisp, sententious and abrupt. He could be flowing with conjunctions and connectives as in this extract from *Of Death*:

> "and therefore a mind fixed and bent upon somewhat that is good doth avert the colours of death. But above all, believe it, the sweetest canticle is, *Nunc dimittis*".

Essays or Counsels, Civil and Moral, is thus, as Hugh Walker writes in *The English Essay and Essayists*:

> "the first true English prose classic".

5

Browne : A Study of Religio Medici

Religio Medici or the Religion of a Doctor is a remarkable book. It was not meant for the public but, as Browne writes *To The Reader* for his "private exercise". Later it was published. Browne was thirty years old when he wrote it in the quiet of Norwich. The seventeenth century was an age of Science with Newton's Laws of motion, the keystone of seventeenth century science as Basil Willy writes in *The Seventeenth Century Background*. A man of science was supposed to have no religion as Science and Religion were opposed. Religion was the basis of scholasticism in the middle ages (The "Science of Being"). Scholastic thought was metaphysical and dealt with Being Essence, Cause and End. The Seventeenth Century was an age of Science and was concerned not with Being but Mechanistic Determinism. Science was thus in contradiction to Religion. Browne was pleading for religion in an age dominated by science.

Browne was a doctor who took his medical degree at Leyden. He had a religion of his own, possessing as Edmund Goose writes, 'an aititude of mind that is scientific and yet reverent'. Browne composed *Religio Medici* to justify himself; the book is his *Apologia* as Newman in the 19th century wrote *Apologia Pro Vita Sua.* It is a personal testimoney, a liberal work in an illiberal age. It is in two parts, the first part consisting of 64 pages and the second of 25 pages. The book is as Browne writes the "Cosmography of Myself".

Browne in the close of The First Part writes of his "singular" nature and his "irregular self". He was an Anglican but his religion was broad-based. It had ideas taken from many sources. He believed in *Origin* and his view that souls are released from torture. Discussing Aristotle he admits "a Trinity of Souls", vegetative, animal, rational. He was inclined to superstition and believed in witches, the burning question of his day found in Reginald Scot's book on Demonology. He held the conceit of *The Arabians* that the souls perished with the body. He accepted the idea of Predestination and Pythagoras's Magic of Numbers. Although an Anglican he was not against those from whom his Christian sect had reformed. He is moved by Roman Catholic ideas. He writes "I could never hear the Ave-Mary bell without an elevation" referring to The Angelus and The Virgin Mary. He believed in prayer for the Dead.

Browne had no system of theology. *Religio Medici* is philosophical. He questioned the fire of Hell. He doubted in the Bible story of Manna as it was gathered in Calabria in Italy or that Eve was created from Adam's rib or that Judas hanged himself of which he wrote there is 'no certainty in Scripture'. All this is in conformity with the seventeenth century which was an Age of Doubt or as John Donne had written: "The new philosophy calls all in doubt".

Browne took his religion, as he writes, not from Rome or Geneva "but the dictates of my own reason". In the first verse which breaks his prose contemplation he writes "Search while thou wilt, and let thy Reason go". He affirms "every man's own reason is his best oedipus" for it can deliver a man as Oedipus delivered Thebes from the riddle of the Sphinx. He gives many 'Theorems of Reason'. He goes beyond Reason too and believes in mystery. He writes "I love to lose myself in a mystery to pursue my Reason to an O altitudo!" or the highest altitude or Wisdom. He believes in Miracles. His faith transcends Reason.

His faith was largely Christian. He writes "all salvation is through Christ". He belives in the Christian belief of the immortality of the soul and rejects the Montpellier theory of vitalism where the soul is an organic part of the fabric of man. He thinks of God as a Metaphysical as Basil Willey writes *The Seventeeth Century Background,* Chapter 3. He has a few theological beliefs like Death, Judgement, Heaven, and Hell. He contemplates the attributes of God, "His Wisdom and Eternity". He considers God in terms of time and the Timeless like T.S. Eliot. Browne writes: "His whole duration being one permanent point without Succession, Parts, Flick, or Division". This is Browne's version of the "Still centre" in Eliots's *Four Quartets.*

He speaks of God in the grandeur of his eloquence. He calls God an Artist, of the Spirit of God as "the fire and scintillation". *The Second Part* ends with his famous "Colloquy with God", first in the verses beginning "The night is come" and second in his final Prayer which ends the book; "Dispose of me according to the wisdom of Thy pleasure: Thy will be done, though in my own undoing".

Browne had a unified sensibility of the metaphysical. He combined science and religion in the Janus or Double Faced Age of the seventeenth century where science and religion are two worlds. As a man of Science he believed in nature. He studied Bees, Ants, Spiders as he finds in them "more curious mathematics". As a doctor he studied the parts of man. He knew astronomy, botany and other science subjects. His work *Christian Morals* is full of scientific imagery. He writes in *Religio Medici* I collect my Divinity from two Books, "one of God, another of his servant Nature". Nature is the "universal and public Manuscript". Analysing Nature and Art he says that both are "servants" of Gods's "Providence". Art is the perfection of nature and "Nature is the Art of God". This is in contrast to what Perdita says in Shakespeare's the Winter's Tale, Act 4, Sc. 4, where art improves on Nature in "streat'd gillyvos" and pied beauty. There are Newtonian ideas in *Religio Medici.* He writes in significantly scientific terminology: "God is like a skilful Geometrician" and has His

"Compass". The whole world runs "not upon an Halix that still enlargeth, but on a Circle".

A feature of *Religio Medici* is the large tolerance or charity of Browne. He never quarrelled with a person for difference of an opinion. He writes "I should violate my own arm rather than a Church". His charity was not only for his own necessity but to "supply the want of others". He gave alms to the poor. He writes of the "Virtue of Charity without which Faith is a mere notion". His medical profession was to cure the patient and when he attended to him he called unto God for his soul. He writes of his constitution which "sympathisest with all things". He had no "Antipathies". He writes: "I am in England everywhere".

He reflects on Man. Man is a Microcosm. He calls Man "that great and true Amphibium" for he can live, as Browne himself did "in divided and distinguished worlds". Every man, he says a double horoscope, one of his "humanity" and another of his "Christianity". He writes of himself: "In philosophy where truth seems double faced there is no man more paradoxical than myself: but in Divinity I love to keep the road". Browne takes the reality of life as he does the reality of Death. He writes "The first day of our Jubilee is Death". He only wants his name in the "Register of God". This is an example of the sublimest contemplation of Browne.

According to Egon Stephen Merton in *Science and Imagination* (1949) Browne had both a "philosophic imagination" which correlates ideas and an "artistic imagination" which relates his ideas to sensation. He writes with melody, tone and rhythm or musical prose, such as, "He sweeteneth the Water with a Wood". *Religio Medici* has sumptuous prose in several parts of the book as he does in the first five paragraphs of the last chapter of *Urn Burial.* What Keats wrote in one of his letters applies to Browne: "Axioms in philosophy are not axioms till they are proved upon our pulses".

6

Nature of Satire

What's satire? Satire is the fine art of calling names. This is a difficult job. It is not easy to call someone by a name which will stick to him for ever. The townsman who purchases a tiny estate in the country is called 'lord of a single lizard' by Juvenal. This is declaiming wittily and sharply. The fine raillery in Horace is equally fascinating. The invective of Juvenal and the raillery of the other are blended in Dryden. This satire is usually directed against some one; still the poem is not made for the person, rather, the person is made for the poem. He shapes it and gives it a unique form. There is, moreover, a tragic satire like that of Juvenal, and there is a comic satire written by Horace. The satirist :

> Charms with graceful negligence,
> And without method talks us into sense.

We are all satirists at some time or other of our lives. The satirist destroys. He is "a demolition expert" like Shaw. It is irrelevant to ask him, what have you constructed? "Shaw's genius", says Tynan, "was for intellectual slum-clearance, not for town-planning". A welfare state, we are convinced, must destroy the slums. But the destruction can be achieved by force or by consent. The satirist believes in the art of persuasion which art is the function of rhetoric. The satirist persuades us to admire or to detest; and the intention distinguishes him from a writer of comedy. To expose, to deride, or to condemn—this is the intention. But in reality there is not much distinction between the earlier comedy and satire. Wycherley's *Plain Dealer* is more a satire and *The Country Wife* is more a comedy. Meredith called his *The Egoist* a comedy, but it reads like a satire. Only the romantic comedy is different from satire. Satire is Kaleidoscopic and volatile.

Butler's *Hudibras*, Pope's Satires, Johnson's *Vanity of Human Wishes*, and Byron's *The Vision of Judgement* are all satires which are critical of actual person and of an actual state of affairs. Here satire becomes indistinguishable from comedy. In both the poets are alive to the follies, faults, and imperfections of men and women. They attack the rigidities, the inelasticity of mind, the lack of adjustment. The writer of a good comedy, however, acts as Counsel for the Defence, while the satirist is Counsel for the Prosecution. As a defender of an authority, he knows no toleration. He is painfully aware of the wide gulf separating what might be from what is. And this makes satire the spontaneous overflow of powerful indignation. Even then it is not what an author has to say that makes it important, but how he says it. Swift's *Modest Proposal* is a good example. It offers a fruitful field of the expanding domain. As Worchester remarked, "the spectrum-analaysis of satire-red runs from the red of invective at one end to the violet of the most delicate irony at the other." In the present century satire is mostly violet, relying on irony, innuendo, and fantasy. The emphasis too has shifted from man to mankind—This is the result of the author's deep faith in the human soul which has to be saved. Thomas Drant said long ago,

> Satire is a tart and carping kind of verse,
> An instrument to pinch the pranks of men.

Then the lines of the satirist must carry with them a tone of authoritative conviction which alone can evoke a compelling consent. Such a feature is implicit in the concentrated couplet.

In the past the people *faultily* derived the word satire from the Greek Satyr, a rough and hairy being. This made them believe that satire must be rugged, abrupt, and violent. Thus you have Donne and Marston. These poets also held that satire must be obscure, and here they probably followed Juvenal and Persius. But outspokenness is really desirable in a satire. When Dryden speaks of the stinginess of Blingby Bathel by saying that :

His Cooks,

Swift admitted that a valid reason for writing a satire must be "the private satisfaction and pleasure of the writer". It is a peculiar pleasure that arises from one's spleen or malice. Still this self-satisfaction invests the satire with some gaiety and recklessness. This is evident in a good satire which usually begins by evoking a confused impression. The author appears to be praising his object. Only slowly do we realize that this praise is really the denigration of the most fatal sort. Such an impression comes from Dryden's *MacFlecknoe*. The values undergo a comic transformation, and the poor Shadwell is taken to pieces :

Shadwell alone my perfect image bears,
Mature in dullness from his tender years.

If we are not convinced, he will tell us that "Shadwell alone" "stands confirmed in full stupidity". Later we read that "Shadwell never deviates into sense". This is a denunciation which is satirical. But any denunciation is not necessarily satirical; it can be the starting point leading to humorous mockery. This would be satirical if the author is detached and the statement is witty and ironical. That is, abuse in itself is not a satire unless it is amplified. The abuse should flow in a torrent drowning the object, and the image must be debasing. It is this that leads the satirist to compose a mock-heroic like *The Rape of the Lock*. The world is niether fully real nor completely unreal. But the wit makes the scene or the situation effective. Thus John Cleveland contemplates the Scots with a sardonic humour and bursts Borth suddenly :

> Had Cain been Scot, God would have changed his doom;
> Not forced him wander but confined him home.

One can relish such a satire if it is of the finest quality. This means that the passage must be charged with strong feeling and disciplined eloquence.

The gregarious, leisured world of persons is apt to be a scandalloving one. Of such a world the product was the Restoration satire. The political satire of this world is always dated and it tends to employ invective. The reader comes halfway to meet the author and appreciate it. Invective too is a form of satire. Charles Churchill speaks of Bishop Warburton as one who :

> Was so proud, that should he meet
> The twelve Apostles in the street,
> He'd turn his nose up at them all,
> And shove his saviour from the wall.

There is a vigour in these lines which shows that the poet was shocked by what he saw and heard. This ability to be shocked depends on the level of the development of the critical faculty.

The satirist then knows what he wants to say even before he begins his composition; and it appears to every one because every man finds his neighbour as the target. As Swift said, "Satire is a sort of glass, wherein beholders do generally discover everybody's face but their own, which is the chief reason for that kind of reception it meets with in the world, and that so very few are offended with it. "The good or successful satirist then seeks to make the reader apply the satire to himself. The impartial reader must be made to see that the satire is not provoked by any malice or prejudice. So Swift puts on an air of assumed carelessness, effectively penetrates the defences of his victim, and seizes every opening. Thus Bickerstaff was laid low. In achieving this end, he makes the reader accept a position which he will not normally take. Once we are in this situation, we are *forced to listen to the* end. Such a position appears in Butler's "colleges of unreason". Referring to the teachers of these colleges, he writes, "I found it difficult to get definite opinions from any of them, except on such subjects as the weather, eating and drinking, holiday excursions, or games of skill. "These professors, he says: "retail" the opinions of others; and they admit *that though "there is an element of truth in what* the writer has said, there are many points on which they are unable to agree with him. Which these points were, I invariably found myself unable to determine". "This" we are told, "is the art of sitting gracefully on a fence", an art which is nowhere "brought to greater perfection than at the Erewhonian colleges of Unreason. "This is devastating, but is it not true *of a large number of our teachers?*

It is true that the satirist sees one aspect of the truth, one aspect of man. He is like an advocate who pleads his case to win our consent, and who therefore has to omit much and exaggerate the little. This over-simplication enables him to have "an absolute dominion over the minds of the spectators" because he makes us blind temporarily, he makes his *sketch look realistic,* and he delights us with his wit. Naturally he refuses to consider the mitigating circumstances. Since he is to put forth his case effectively, he magnifies, belittles or distorts the picture. This imposes a strain upon the reader whose imaginative co-operation is required. Thus Dryden takes up Shaftesbury as if the latter is sitting for a portrait. There are many ludicrous possibilities attaching to such a person. Dryden begins with these and proceeds to a total denunciation of the sitter :

A Vermin wriggling in th' usurper's ear,
Bart'ring his Venal wit for sums of gold,
He cast himself into the Saintlike mould;
Graned, sighed, and prayed, while Godliness was gain,
The lewdest Bagpipe of the Squeaking train.

These hammer blows fall successively with no interval. They fall so rapidly that no time is given for a recovery. This personal satire is the result of the need for revenge for a personal affront, and of the awareness of the man becoming a public nuisance. At the same time the true satirist, as Dryden was, has a sense of proportion. This would imply that the satirist avoids the extremes and seeks to convince us that he is right.

7

Gray's Melancholy : A Viewpoint

The strain of melancholy in the poetry of Gray has *baffled the critics. His contemporary Dr. Johnson calls him* "a dull fellow"[1]. Doughty[2] and Arnold[3] believe that the age was not congenial to his spirits. Doughty also partly believes that death of his friend, Richard West and other relations in quick succession was the reason for his melancholy[4]. Gosse explaining the nature of his melancholy says that probably a "*judicious medical treatment*"[5] *might have removed this* strain. Ketton-Cremèr does not believe with Gosse. He only points out that his melancholy is "a trouble of the spirit"[6].

The views quoted above are highly misleading. Dr. Johnson and Gray had strained relation which accounts for the offensive and unfair language he used for the poet. *Doughty seems to believe that mere age and death are the sole* factors responsible for his melancholy which they are not. Arnold thinks of the possibility of putting Gray side by side either "with Milton" or "Burns"[7] which is too stupendous a job for anybody to accomplish. Gosse should have referred to `psychistric instead of to medical treatment, but it was *uncommon in his days. Ketton-Cremer's statement sounds* more or less like an epigram, and it is highly ambiguous.

The Strain of Melancholy in Gray's Writings

Melancholy is "an inbred malady"[8] and a certain strain of it is present in all of us Gray has an overdose of melancholy and hence the question: "Why is he a Melancholy Man?"

A mood of diffused sorrow descended on the poet when he was an adolescent student. He termed Tibullus to be his "favourite elegiac poet" in his letter of December 22, 1736[9] to Richard West, adding that "so melancholy a poesie" was congenial to his "low spirits and constant ill health." He found himself a misfit in the company of boys with mirthful spirits and boyish vigour. Again writing to the same friend on August 22, 1737, he stated that, "Low spirits are my true and faithful companions; they get up with me, go to bed with me, make journeys and returns as I do; nay and pay visits, and will even affect to be jocose, and force a feeble laugh with me . . . ."[10] Another letter of May 27, 1742, to the same friend reveals a further deepening of the strain of melancholy. He wrote, "Mine you are to know is a white melancholy, or rather Leucocholy for the most part; which though it seldom laughs or dances, nor ever amounts to what one calls Joy or Pleasure, yet is a good easy sort of state. . . . "[11] In the earlier letter it was like a constant companion with which he could even afford to be happy. But here it gets into his blood and becomes a part of his personality. Cool wisdom dawns upon him through experience and long association with melancholy and he realises that it can seldom give him "Joy or Pleasure". In his characteristic humorous way he terms his melancholy to be "white" "or rather leucocholy". The word "Leucocholy" may cause some difficulty to a casual reader. But it can be safely asserted that it is Gray's coinage from the word "Leucocyte" which means "a white corpuscle of the blood . . . ."[12] The term "white melancholy" further bears out the point. He coins the word "Leucocholy" to describe his melancholy. The word suggests that the strain of melancholy is so deep-rooted in him that it is, more or less, an indispensable part of his mental and spiritual make-up. It has become one with his blood, just as the white corpuscles are an indispensable part of human blood. The word "Leucocholy" in addition to describing adequately Gray's melancholy satisfies his poetic ear too, as it rhymes well with melancholy.

During his stay at Stoke Pogis in the spring of 1742 he was visited by an unusual poetic inspiration, for in quick succession he composed four poems.[13] In 'Ode on Spring' he chose to talk a good deal about his personal problems under the cover of spring.

"Contrasting the well-remembered happiness of his school-days with the melancholy of his present life, he came to write his 'Ode on a Distant Prospect of Eton College'.[14] The mere fact that the boys at Eton are men is sufficient to justify and ensure their suffering. The note of melancholy touches the supreme depths in the last stanza of the poem. With intense morbidity and sincerity of feelings the poet sings in the "last lovely stanza":[15]

"To each his sufferings, all are men
    Condemned alike to groan,
The tender for another's pain,
    The unfeeling for his own.
Yet ah! why should they know their fate?
Since sorrow never comes too late,
    And happiness too swiftly flies".

Gray's spirit at the time was considerably weighed down by West's death and his estrangement from Walpole. He was, naturally, tortured by a sense of loneliness which stirred the deep-rooted melancholy in him and as a result of this we have this song of utter depression and hopelessness. The poem clearly indicates Gray's "sense of insecurity, the apprehensiveness, the fear of illness and pain which were to haunt him throughout his life."[16] It is evident that the poem is deeply personal and the poet finds a very pathetic contrast as the grown up Gray visualises with his mind's eye the boy Gray when he was "a stranger yet to pain."[17]

The 'Hymn to Adversity' is not acutely pessimistic as the 'Eton Ode' happens to be. Doughty says, "The bitterness of the pessimism is softened by a recognition of the moral values of sorrow. The poet's mind is a dark cloud, but it is a cloud touched with silver".

The '*Sonnet on the Death of Richard West*' is purely an expression of personal grief directly as opposed to the poems mentioned above where he relates his private sorrows in the garb of wider philosophic issue so that they may appear as the universal lot of man.

His most famous poem the 'Elegy' written in a Country Churchyard is really a bewailing cry. He was variously shocked before starting to write this poem. His well-known quarrel[18] with Walpole and the four bereavements that he had suffered—namely, his uncle Roger's death, father's death, West's death and aunt Mary Antrobus's death had shaken him considerably. The shock drew from the poet a song, and the deeper the intensity of it, the more melodious was the song. In the 'Elegy', Gray is talking about his own personal problems under this or that pretext. And, indeed, "the addition of the final fifty-two lines was an attempt to depersonalise the poem.[19] The "Village-Hampden"[20], or the "inglorious Milton", or the "Cromwell guiltless of his country's blood" is Gray himself. He was, indeed, "a Youth to Fortune and to Fame unknown."[21] At some places he laments over his lot, at others he gets reconciled to it by pointing out that even obscurity has its advantages.[22]

Even in the famous Pindaric Ode, 'The Progress of Poesy', where his inspiration is purely classical, the strain of melancholy finds expression:

> "Man's feeble race what ills awit,
> Labour, and Penury, the racks of Pain,
> Disease and Sorrow's weeping train,
> And Death, sad refuge from the storms of
> Fate!"

The strain of melancholy, which descended upon his spirits so early in life, did not decrease with the advancing age. His "Journal in the Lakes", written in the form of letters to Dr. Wharton describing the scenic beauty of the Lake

District just two years before his death, has touches of melancholy and solitary broodings.

Bonstetten, a Swiss young man, who became very fond of Gray, towards the fag-end of the poet's life (and whom Gray also liked immensely), has recorded that, "He was the most melancholy and gentlemanlike of poets."[23]

It is, thus, clear that the strain of melancholy was an inseparable companion of Gray. This deep strain naturally clamoured for expression and found it frequently and invariably in whatever he happened to write—letters, poems or journal.

It is, perhaps, the deep strain of melancholy which makes him shun worldly fame and greatness. It is well-known that he never desired that his poems should be published, or if they were at all published, he preferred to remain anonymous. This was the reason why he refused to give his approval for publication to his greatest poem the 'Elegy'[24] and quietly refused laureateship when it was offered to him in 1757.

Writing eases the tension within the people. The Muse was a safety valve to him. He wrote in one of his letters to Dr. Wharton, "The Muse, I doubt is gone, and has left me in far worse company." The age-factor emphasised by Doughty and Arnold assumes importance when one considers the scantiness of Gray's publication. He was swayed by conflicting literary influences. He was a lover of both Dryden and Spenser. He, thus, in the words of a critic "oscillates between Spenser and Dryden, between romantic feeling and imagination on the one hand, and classic restraint on the other."

The Possible Reasons for the Strain of Melancholy

Bonstteten thought that Gray's melancholy was due to the fact that he never loved, and obviously love he meant the natural course of love culminating in a happy marriage. Bonstetten became very intimate with Gray towards the fag-end of his life and his estimate of Gray is dependable after a careful analysis.

Some significant lines in the 'Ode on Spring' may be referred to. Contrasting his miserable lot with the joys of spring season, the poet addresses his ownself and sings:

> "Poor moralist! and what art thou?
> A solitary fly!
> Thy joys no glittering female meets,
> No hive hast thou of hoarded sweets,
> No painted plumage to display;
> On hasty wings thy youth is flown,
> Thy sun is set thy spring is gone . . . ."[25]

To me it appears that Gray sums up the various factors that culminated in his melancholy. Gray betrays a great longing for a "glittering female" as life-partner and a sweet hive. In the absence of the long cherished desire, which remains unfulfilled, he feels utterly disgusted and compares himself to "a solitary fly" which is destined to misfortune and disappointment. He was neither a successful man nor was he a great poet.

Yet in another poem written earlier than 'Ode on Spring' he gives vent to somewhat similar feelings. It is a Latin poem and runs thus:

> " . . . . Salve vocanti rite, fesso et
> Da placidam juveri quietem
> Quod si invidendis sedious, et frui
> Fortune sacra lege silentil
> Vetat volentem, me resorbeus
> In medics violenta fluctus,
> Saltem remoto des, Pater, angulus
> Horas senectae ducere liberas;
> Tutumque vulgari tumultu
> Surripias, hominumque curis."[26]

The lines may be rendered in English as follows:

> "Be gracious to him who calls thus solemnly upon Thee, and grant repose to soothe his young but weary head.

> And if fate yields not to my longing for that happy home, where silence rules by divine decree, sucking me rudely back into the mid-waves of the world, grant Father, this at least that when I am grown old I may in some secluded corner lead a life that is truly mine, and withdraw me safe away from the tumult of the crowd and the cares that vex mankind."[27]

Obviously, Gray gave his first choice to a "happy home where silence rules by divine decree, "but unfortunately Fate granted him the second, i.e., "some secluded corner . . ." in "the Arctic Pole of Cambridge" where "he felt his heart to be frozen."[28]

Evidently, though he had a longing for a happy family life, he lacked the necessary worldly habit to take positive steps towards the realisation of that object the negation of which he felt so keenly. An overdose of melancholy is too prone to make a person inactive in the worldly sense of the term.

It has been argued that there is a tone of melancholy in most of the poets of the eighteenth century, but such precise and poignant references to the poet's own private sorrows are not present in any one of them.

Gray and Miss Speed

A loving soul that Gray was, it is really surprising that he could not love and marry. Even when an opportunity came he let it slip by. In the Manor house of Stoke, there lived Lady Cobham with Lady Schaub, a French woman, and Miss Henrietta Jane Speed, "a lively and attractive young woman of twenty-two."[29] Lady Cobham discovered that the author of the 'Elegy' was living so close to her and sent the two ladies to him. When they came, Gray was out and they left behind a formal slip.

The strain in which the episode has been celebrated by the poet in his poem 'A Long Story' is eloquent of the fact that Gray was much influenced by it. On the surface of it, it reads like a trifle. It was customary with Gray to give such a twist to a situation as to create laughter. But this "natural and original turn" (Walpole)[30] of humour does not take away the gravity and sincerity of the emotion which characterises the poem. As a matter of fact there was nothing poetic about the visit of the two ladies or the slip that they had left behind which Gray described as a "spell".[31] The very fact that he squeezed poetry out of this event bears out the contention that it was not the critic, but he alone who felt it to be a romantic episode and was touched by it. The call of the two ladies has been humorously described by the poet as a military invasion. While describing Lady Schaub, he was fully alive to the "art of killing"[32] of polished and bewitching young women; but while referring to the other lady, Miss Speed, Gray begins to have some breathing of the heart and his voice melts into raptures. He showers encomiums upon her. The stanza is marked by a genuineness of emotion and truly "a Cypress, not a bosom, hideth"[33] the heart of the poet:

"To celebrate her eyes, her air,
    Coarse panegyrics whould but tease her.
Melissa is her nom de gurre:
    Alas, who would not wish to please her."[34]

Melissa, the name given to Miss Speed, means a "beneficent fairy."[35] The last line is the very assence of what Gray genuinely felt about her. The poet acknowledges the captivating power of the fair sex to which was, probably, not alive or exposed till that hour:

"Short was his joy. He little knew
    The power of Magic was not fable;
Out of the window, whisk, they flew,
    But left a spell upon the table."[36]

He talks about his first visit to Manor House in the form of a criminal trial and soon discovers that his terror of the ladies was meaningless, for the lady "smiled and bid him come to dinner."

Though it is a poem full of humour and gaiety, it is not difficult to trace in it some real warmth of emotion through the delightful surface of the poem which Gray used as a covering. The poem depicts unmistakably—in spite of the apparent tone—Gray's longing for a happy home and a "glittering female" which he had voiced in 'Ode on Spring' and the absence of the long cherished object he carried to heart. It was rather "Melancholy" affecting "to be jocose" and it actually did "force a feeble laugh with" him.

Miss Speed warmly acknowledged 'A Long Story' by her letter[37] of October, 1750, to Gray. The other letters[38] of Miss Speed which is extent, has a much more intimate tone than the earlier one. Gray had, probably, made a lover's usual complaint of her lukewarm love for him. In reply to this, she earnestly convinced him that he, unfortunately, did not know her "Tear" otherwise he would have been "content with it, but knowing my exterior so well as you do you can easily conceive me Vain of the Partiality you show me . . . ." Certainly a young girl of a respectable family and living with a respectable kith and kin would not talk of "heart" to a young man if he were not intimate to her. In the same letter she reveals a great concern about his health and a burning impatience to have his company. After all this anxiety and talk about health, the lady uses "the Strongest argument to tempt" the poet to come:

" . . . . . indeed I can make use of the Strongest argument to tempt you which is that at this time it will be a deed of Charity as we are absolutely alone." The letter closes with a very intimate assurance to serve him *in a perfect manner*.

The extracts from the letter quoted above are self-explanatory and denote quite clearly that the relationship between them—to say the least—was very warm and intimate. After quoting some of the relevant extracts from the letter of Miss Speed to Gray, one naturally feels Mr. Ketton-Cremer that ". . . . enough has been quoted to show the affection and solicitude with which she had now come to regard Gray."[39]

But it will be worthwhile to mention some of the relevant facts regarding the issue. During the summer of 1760 and nearabout it, Gray passed a few months in the very close company of Miss Speed. Lady Cobham died with Gray and Miss Speed by her bed-side and it was naturally rumoured that they were to be united for ever shortly after Lady Cobham's death.

Sometime later, Miss Speed and Gray went on to stay with Miss Speed's old friend Mrs. Jennings at Grovelands near Shiplake in Oxfordshire. Only Mrs. Jennings, a middle aged widow and her daughter, Susannah were living there.[40] This was the fittest occasion for Gray and Miss Speed to have developed an intimate kind of relationship which, probably, they could not do earlier. Ketton-Cremer rightly remarks that "If the attachment between Gray and Henrietta Speed could ever have developed into something more, this might have proved the time and the place—the sunny days and long twilight evenings of July, in a house of chosen friends, set on a hill whose wooded slopes fell steeply to a noble reach of the Thames."[41] The three lidies i.e., Mrs. Jennings, her daughter Susannah and Miss Speed were very nice to him and actually "wore my spirits"[42] as Gray wrote to Dr. Wharton on October 21, 1760.

It is clear from the above observations on the relationship between Gray and Miss Speed that each regarded the other not only with a sense of strong admiration but with a degree of emotional attachment reaching practically the domain of reciprocal love. In view of this, it is indeed difficult to say as to what could be the possible reason or reasons which proved to be so insurmountable as not to allow the two loving souls to get together for ever. It will not only be unjust, but solely incorrect to say that Gray by temperament was incapable of the feeling of love. Besides the boyhood friendships which are famous as a "quadruple alliance,"[43]he could form very affactionate friendships—some of them much later in his life—with Nicholls, Bonstetten, Robinson, Wharton, Stonehewer and Brown. Bonstetten and Nicholls had a very great respect and affection for him. Both of them, with many others, were violently shocked at his passing away. Nicholls has gone on record with a significant remark, "I considered Mr. Gray as a second Parent . . . ."[44]

Gray was even quite capable of loving a woman. From his pen-portrait of Miss Speed in 'A Long Story' even a casual reader would, naturally, gather the impression that she was most beautiful. But Earl Harcourt in his character-sketch of Miss Speed says, "Her person tall, but not slender, her complexion dark, and although she had *no pretensions to beauty*, yet an easy and graceful air with fine eyes and teeth, united to render her *altogether extremely pleasing*...."[45] Evidently, Gray mixed up his feelings with the pen-portrait of Miss Speed in 'A Long Story'.

Some Personal Experiences

Normally Gray should have married Miss Speed, but it appears that something was wrong either with Gray or with Miss Speed or with both. In order to get at this, which is purely a personal issue, one will have to take into account the private life of the persons concerned—specially the early life of Gray. The strongest single influence on the mental make up of a child is that of his parents, were not able to get on well together. His father, Philip Gray, has been described by critics as a clever, but extravagant businessman, violent, jealous and probably mad. He might have been a practical businessman, but he was never a balanced sort of person. He did not care at all for his children and refused to educate Gray, the only surviving child out of the twelve. The relationship between the poet's father and mother was most lamentable. This is evidenced by a case submitted for the Counsel's opinion by the poet's mother, Dorothy Gray for the possibilities of a judicial separation. In this extra-ordinary document the poet's mother alleged that the poet's father "used her in the most inhuman manner, by beating, kicking, punching, and with the most abusive language, that she hath been in the utmost fear and danger of her life . . . ."[46] She went on to state that the poet's father was determined to "pursue her with all the vengeance possible, and will ruin himself to render her, and his only son."[47] Since such a separation was not possible according to the Counsel's opinion, some sort of forced reconciliation took place between them. Obviously, it was a sort of marriage where though the flesh joined, the spirit was at war and the terrible emotional disturbance and a sense of insecurity—to which the early financial trouble naturally contributed its share—must have been experienced by the sensitive child, Thomas Gray, who was passing through an impressionable phase of his life. The impressions gathered in the infancy are never obliterated. The storm that is let loose by a cruel fate upon an individual from the earlier days of his infancy, influences his attitude throughout his whole life.

Gray was tossed by conflicting influences so far his attitude to women was concerned. On the one hand he had his own loving mother, Dorothy; on the other his bosom friend, West's mother, who was cruel to her son and insincere to her husband. Dorothy, the poet's mother, was really a loving mother. Gray was attached to her very much. She actually arranged for the poet's education at Eton, when he was a little more than ten with the help of her two brothers, namely, Robert Antrobus and Thomas Antrobus. The thought of his mother was a constant companion of the poet during his Continental tour with Horace Walpole and he frequently wrote long letters to her. Mother had none else to love except the child and it is often natural for mothers to direct their starved affections towards their children. Mother is the first woman a boy comes in contact with in his life and his outlook on women in general is shaped by the influence exercised by the mother over him.

The next woman who influenced Gray's attitude towards women was literally next to his mother. She was his dear friend West's mother, who was a woman of dubious moral character and was such a wretch that even his son doubted her fidelity towards his father, which, as Gray believed in all seriousness, hastened West's death when he was in the prime of his manhood. It was nobody else but West himself who disclosed this ghastly secret to Gray. Edmund Gosse states :

"In extreme agitation West confided to his friend a terrible secret which he had disclosed, and which Gray preserved in silence until the close of his life, when he told it to Norton Nicholls. It is a painful story which need not be repeated here, but which involved the reputation of West's mother with the name of his late father's secretary, Mr. (John) Williams, whom she finally married when her son was dead."[48]

The very fact that West could reveal such a top personal secret which compromised his mother's reputation, is eloquent of the very deep-rooted affection that existed between the two. The friendship formed at Eton College at the innocent age of ten, naturally, developed into the strongest brotherly affection. Hence it is no exaggeration to say that Gray looked upon West's mother only as next to his own.

Three Factors

Thus the personal experiences of Gray were not only unfortunate and sad but were extremely abnormal. These experiences were drawing him towards the kind of life that he actually led. It should be noted that the three factors mentioned in the preceding lines had their inevitable impact on Gray's personality.

Firstly, he must have carried a vivid, awe-inspiring memory of the trouble between his parents, and probably, developed an aversion to marriage. Born of a very abnormal wedlock and abandoned by his father, he had been deprived of the loving home atmosphere that would have helped him create a similar atmosphere by marrying himself.

Secondly, the excessive fondness for his mother was not conducive to marriage either. There was no wonder that he was looking for a *mother* in the girls whom he met. Mr. H.W. Hepner, a famous modern American psychologist, has put the idea well as follows :

"When a mother hugs and kisses her small boy far more than she does her husband, she may be conditioning her child for a bachelorship or for a troublesome married life."[49]

Judged from the motherly standard the girls failed miserably and Gray concluded against them :

"What female heart can gold despise ?"
What cat's averse to fish ?"[50]

Thirdly, the ghastly revelation of the objectionable moral character of West's mother must have driven Gray away from women and he must have formed a very poor opinion of them.

As a grown up man, consciously Gray pined for a "glittering female" and a "hive" of "hoarded sweets", and felt even passing pleasure in the company of Miss Speed. So far as the ego is concerned it is absolutely normal. But it should be remembered that a man, who has undergone bitter experiences, is bound to retain a very vivid impression of these experiences throughout his life which adversely affect the unconscious side of his personality.

The very complex personal experiences were responsible for the fact that though Gray was instinctively drawn towards Miss Speed, he was not really serious about marriage. In 'A Long Story' itself, Gray, while admiring Miss Speed's beauty says, "Alas, who would not wish to please her". Why should he insert the word 'Alas' in this context which seems to be out of place? The above poem reveals in a symbolical manner the poet's terror of a married life. He ran away from the two female warriors, although the only punishment they wanted to inflict upon the poet was to invite him to dinner.

The fact—that he was drawn towards Miss Speed, but was not serious about marriage—has been further borne out by some letters which he wrote to Dr. Wharton during the time. Just one significant extract from Gray's letter of August, 1758 will be referred to here. In July, 1758 Gray stayed with Lady Cobham and Miss Speed in London and later wrote to Dr. Wharton a very ambiguous line that he (Gray) would have gladly stayed (at Lady Cobham's place) longer "but for the reason we talked about."[51] The reason could not be anything else, but "as Tovey suggested, that Gray is alluding to his fear of Lady Cobham wishing to make match between Gray and Miss Speed."[52]

Gray's reaction to the marriage of his once sweetheart is worth quoting. On January 11, 1761, he wrote to Dr. Wharton :

"My old friend Miss Speed has done what the World calls a very foolish thing. She has married the Baron de la

Peyriere. . . .he is about 28 years old[53] (ten years younger than herself) but looks nearer 40. This is not the effect of debauchery, for he is a very sober Man; good-natured and honest, and no Conjuror."[54]

The letter is marked by the general coldness of Gray towards Miss Speed. One cannot do better than quote the comments of Ketton-Cremer on the above extract :

"In any case Henrietta Speed mattered little to him now. She had brought a measure of warmth and gaiety into his life for a few years, none was always grateful to her and wished her well."[55]

And yet, while talking of Miss Speed's husband, one smells a lovers's heart in Gray. The "expression 'no Conjuror' was applied in eighteenth century to persons of less than average intelligence;"[56] and, this expression he used for her husband.

Gray met Miss Speed as Madame de la Peyriere in London four years after her marriage and fifteen years after the composition of 'A Long Story'. Later he wrote to Dr. Wharton that she was "exceeding glad to see me and I"[57] her.

Ketton-Cremer, again, comments, "It was a happy meeting, with no regrets on either side for the past: but Madame de la Payriere does not appear in Gray's life or in his letters"[58] after this.

A Lonely Man

Gray was, indeed, a lonely man, given to solitude and its charms right from the very beginning, so much so that he started feeling a sort of kinship with it. In his own words he was "a solitary fly". Such brooding loneliness is strewn in most of his letters and poems. The 'Elegy' is nothing but the depiction of the solitary sojourn of the poet, in the countryside round about the Stoke Pogis Churchyard busy in his own sad reflections.

Evidently—though Gray had numerous near and dear friends—he was essentially a lonely man. Miss Speed must have smelt this and it is difficult to say whether she made earnest efforts to convince Gray that a change for a life of close and intimate companionship—full of the warmth of love and emotional harmony—would really be a change for the better; or that Gray with his wavering love for Miss Speed—sometimes warm and at other times lukewarm—"sailed into the north" of his "lady's opinion".[59] Whatever may be Miss Speed's attitude towards Gray, it is clear that she could not overcome Gray's very many apprehensions to marriage. Lord Harcourt records about Miss Speed, "In truth she was as incapable of the feelings of affection as of those of hatred or dislike; she could extract entertainment even from folly or insipidity, and no company displeased her, but she really loved nobody."[60] In view of the warm and affectionate letter of the 25th August, 1759, that Miss Speed had written to Gray, it is difficult to say whether Lord Harcourt's estimate of Miss Speed is literally true. However, it may have certain amount of truth. "A more normal woman, genuinely in love with him, might conceivably have overcome his fundamental indifference to her sex, the barriers of shyness and reserve with which he had excluded all strong emotion from his life. But they could never be overcome by Henreitta Speed; and there was to be no other woman in his life. 'Thy joys no glittering female meets'. . . . He had written the prophetic words almost twenty years before in the 'Ode on Spring'; and they remained true until the end."[61]

Gray gratified Miss Speed's ambition to 'possess something from his pen on the subject of love'. He produced a mechanical and insipid little song whose very dullness in comparison with the high spirits of 'A Long Story' suggests the stagnation into which their relationship had drifted :

"Midst Beauty and Pleasure's gay triumphs, to languish
And droop without knowing the source of my anguish:
To start from short slumbers, and look for the morning—
Yet close my dull eyes when I see it returning :
Sighs sudden and frequent, looks ever dejected,
Sounds that steal from my tongue, by no meaning
connected:
Ah say, Fellow-swains, how these symptoms be fell me ?

They smile and reply not.
Sure Delia will tell me !"[62]

Whatever may be the drawbacks of the poem, it clearly depicts the poet's deep-rooted melancholy which makes him shut his eyes to "Beauty and Pleasure's gay triumphs". Miss Speed must have realised by now "that there could be no question of marriage between them,"[63] and since she could not have love from him, she at least wanted, to 'possess something from his pen on the subject of love', but the cold gales of melancholy had frozen his heart to which the above poem bears an eloquent witness. He was in a state of mental conflict, because he was torn between the normal desire for a mate and the factors which prevented the realisation of that. An expert on the subject says, "Freud studied many cases of nervous disorders and was convinced that the main cause or impulse was, he believed, of sexual nature". Melancholy and brooding habits tend to weaken a man's capacity to face the actual problems of life and to take a quick decision. Besides, Gray, by nature, was overcautious and avoided taking the least of risk. Gray's house had been destroyed by fire in May, 1748. He not only got his houses insured through Wharton,[64] but desired of him to buy a rope-ladder with strong hooks at the top in January, 1756. Gray got an iron bar fixed to a window of his room on the second floor at Peterhouse which is still there. These arrangements attracted great attention. Some mischievous "fellow-commoners", one night in February, 1756 alarmed the poet with a cry of fire. "Gray without staying to put on his clothes, hooked his rope-ladder to the iron bar, and descended nimbly into the tub of water, from which he was rescued with shouts of laughter by the unmannerly youths."[65] It appears that there was "a deep capacity for brutal folly underneath the varnish of the eighteenth century."[66]

Gray's Adjustment with Melancholy

Melancholy, thus, was deep-rooted in the very personality of Gray and all his life he tried to get adjusted with it. To function is the chief motive of life. No living being can ever remain inactive. A man, naturally is active at all hours, whether he is sleeping, thinking, resting, playing, working or day-dreaming. Even dying is an activity after which there is the complete negation of all activity. It is not to be wondered at that Gray's response to his environment was not always adequate and healthy. The ravages of fate had been last loose on him right from the days of his infancy. Obviously his psychic habits had but short time to develop and as a child he found himself "under the necessity of orientating himself to the unchangeable conditions of actuality, while his technique of adjustment was still immature."[67] There is nothing to be surprised at if Gray developed a feeling of kinship with melancholy, since it was a sort of constant companion to him right from the earliest days.

Shock had shaken Wordsworth so violently that he ceased to sing for sometime. It was quite otherwise with Gray. Misfortune did not come to him as a mere shock. It did not draw from him the usual emotional response of anxiety. The strain of melancholy was already ever present in him in abundance and it had gone deep into the very shaping of his personality. It was Gray's melancholy and nobody could have separated the man from it. The way he received a shock and responded to it was peculiar. He had been used to it Shock simply stimulated the melancholy which was already there, which in its turn inspired the poet to sing a song. He sang whenever his melancholy was intensified by some new shock. He wrote poems not to complain of his miserable lot, but to present a picture of life as he saw and experienced it.

Gray could not have lived with his melancholy all the time looming large, though it was his "true and faithful companion". He must, at times, be needing some kind of relaxation. Sometimes he tries to escape from the world of grim reality into the world of his childhood. When the problem of his present is too stupendous for a man to solve in a satisfactory manner, he regresses mentally to a former happier state when life was more satisfying. He does it in 'Eton Ode' where he celebrates the days of his innocent boyhood. He was then "a stranger yet to pain".

This was how Gray tried to get adjusted with his

melancholy. He could not help it. He must somehow try to adjust himself to his world until death overtakes him and shatters the process of adjustment. Thus, Gray, who has become a prince among elegists with practically a single 'Elegy' that he has composed, had very extraordinary personal experiences—giving rise to and aggravating his melancholy. Critics have written much on "The Elegy written in a Country Churchyard" without caring to analyse the factors which shaped the mental and spiritual make-up of the man who was to become the poet of the 'Elegy'—immortal song which "exercised an influence on all the poetry of Europe, from Denmark to Italy, from French to Russia. With the exception of certain works of Byron and Shakespeare no English poem has been so widely admired and imitated abroad."[68]

Thus a picture of Gray that emerges from a perusal of his life, letters, journal and poetry is not a very vigorous or a happy one. He is a Melancholy Man. The age and other outer factors may have contributed to it, but what is important is the fact that Gray's melancholy had its roots in purely personal causes. He was acutely aware of conflict and unrest within himself.

REFERENCES

1. Williams, W.T. & Vallins, G.H. (Ed.) : 'Gray Collins and their Circle', London, 1937, p. 131.
2. Doughty, O.: 'English Lyric in the Age of Reason', 1922, p. 163.
3. Arnold, M.: 'Thomas Gray' (well-known essay).
4. Doughty, O.: 'English Lyric in the Age of Reason'.
5. Gosse, E.: 'Gray', London, 1889, p. 13.
6. Ketton-Cremer, R.W. : 'Thomas Gray', London, 1955, p. 66.
7. Arnold, M.: 'Thomas Gray'.
8. Burton, R.: 'Anatomie Melancholy'.
9. Toynbee, P. & Whibley, L.: 'Correspondence of Thomas Gray', Vol. I, London, 1935, p. 58.

10. Ibid., p. 66.
11. Ibid., p. 209.
12. "Chamber's Twentieth Century Dictionary", 1948, p. 523.
13. (a) 'Ode on Spring; (b) 'Eton Ode'; (c) 'Hymn to Adversity; (d) 'Sonnet on the Death of Richard West'.
14. Ketton-Cremer, R.W. : 'Thomas Gray', p. 62.
15. Ibid., p. 63.
16. Ibid.
17. 'Ode on a Distant Prospect of Eton College', 1.14.
18. During their Continental tour at Reggio the two friends, namely, Gray and Walpole quarrelled in May, 1741, probably over a trifling matter of a letter which was addressed to Gray, but Walpole opened it. Gray was obliged to stop the journey and return home.
19. Bateson, F.W. : 'English Poetry', London, 1950, p. 187.
20. 'The Elegy Written in a Country Churchyard', 11.57-60.
21. Ibid., 1.118.
22. Ibid., 11.66-72.
23. "On Feb. 10, 1751, the editors of the 'Magazine of Magazines' asked for permission to print it (Elegy). Gray refused and at once wrote to Walpole asking him to publish anonymously" (Poole, A.L. (Ed.): 'The Poems of Gray & Collins', London, 1950, p. 89.
24. Gosse, E.: 'Gray', p. 198.
25. 'Ode on Spring', 11.43-49.
26. Ketton-Cremer, R.W. : 'Thomas Gray', p. 51.
27. Ibid.
28. Gosse, E.: 'Gray', p. 198.
29. Ketton-Cremer, R. W. : 'Thomas Gray', p. 103.
30. Ibid., p. 104.
31. 'A Long Story', p. 1.80.
32. Ibid., 1.28.
33. Shakespeare, W.: 'The Twelfth Night', III, i, 11.136-37.
34. 'A Long Story', 11.29-36.
35. Williams, W.T. & Vallins, G.H. (Ed.); Gray, Collins and their Circle, p. 147.
36. 'A Long Story', 11.77-80.
37. Toynbee, P. & Whibley, L.: 'Correspondence of Thomas Gray', Vol. I, pp. 331-334.
38. Ibid., Vol. II, pp. 636-638.
39. Ketton-Cremer, R.W. : 'Thomas Gray', p. 171.
40. Ibid., p. 703. (Facts in the two sentences borrowed from).
41. Ibid.
42. Toynbee, P. & Whibley, L. : 'Correspondence of Thomas Gray', Vol. II, p. 703.
43. The name given by general approval of all the members to a circle of friends of which Gray was a member. The other three were Horace Walpole, Richard West and Thomas Ashton.

44. Gosse, E.: 'Gray', p. 209.
45. Ketton-Cremer, R.W. : 'Thomas Gray', p. 173.
46. Gosse, E : 'Gray', p. 9.
47. Ketton-Cremer, R.W. : 'Thomas Gray', p. 17.
48. Gosse, E.: 'Gray', p. 47.
49. Hepner, H.W. : 'Psychology applied to Life and Works'.
50. 'Ode on the Death of a Favourite Cat', 11.23-24.
51. *Toynbee, P. & Whibley, L.: 'Correspondence of Gray'*, Vol. II, p. 578.
52. Ibid.
53. Miss Speed "was nearly 34 and her husband was 24' 'Ketton-Cremer : 'Thomas Gray', p. 185.
54. Toynbee P. & Whibley, L. (Ed.) : 'Correspondence of Thomas Gray', Vol. II, p. 770.
55. Ketton-Cremer, K.W.: 'Thomas Gray', p. 185.
56. Ibid
57. Toynbee, P. & Whibley, L. (Ed.) : 'Correspondence of Thomas Gray' Vol. III, p.923.
58. *Ketton-Cremer, R.W.: 'Thomas Gray'*, p. 214.
59. Shakespeare, W.: 'The Twelfth Night', III, ii, 11, 11-12.
60. Ketton-Cremer, R.W.: 'Thomas Gray', p. 173.
61. Ibid., p. 174.
62. *Ibid.*
63. Ibid., p. 175.
64. Gosse, E.: 'Gray', p. 14 (Facts borrowed from).
65. Ibid., p. 125.
66. Ibid.
67. Adler, Afred : 'Understanding Human Nature!
68. Gosse, E.: 'Gray', p. 97.

8

Tennyson: "Ulysses"

At first sight a simple poem. Ulysses, after ten years of war at Troy, and ten more of baffled wandering, has struggled home at last to his rugged Ithaca, off the western coast of Greece. But the sea-rover cannot rest. His wife, he says (somewhat ungallantly), is aged; his people gross; he will leave them to his prudent heir Telemachus, and venture with his old comrades on a last voyage—out into the waste Atlantic. What has life worth living for, but new knowledge, fresh experience?

For Tennyson, however, the poem contained deeper, symbolic meanings. In 1828-29 at Trinity College, Cambridge, he had formed a passionate friendship with Arthur Hallam from Eton, son of Hallam the historian. In 1830 the pair travelled to the Pyrenees with funds for Spanish insurgents; in 1831 Hallam became engaged to Tennyson's sister Emily; but in September 1833, at Vienna, he suddenly died.

Never perhaps has a poet devoted so much time and space to mourning a dead friend. For the wraith of Hallam is present in "The Two Voices" (1833-4), where hope argues with despair; in the lyric "Break, break, break"; in the 131 sections of "In Memoriam", built up through seventeen years (1833-50); and here in "Ulysses" (begun 1833) which, said Tennyson, "gave my feeling about the need of going forward and braving the struggle of life".

He could not expect his readers to divine that; but, for full appreciation, the poem does demand some knowledge of its twin sources—Homer and Dante.

Homer's Odysseus, long kept from reaching home by the anger of the sea-god Poseidon, was bidden by Circe the sorceress to ask counsel of the dead prophet Tiresias gave it and added, mysteriously:

> For thyself Death from the sea shall rise,
> Most peacefully, when a calm old age weighs down thine eyes
> Amidst thy happy people. (*Odyssey*, XI, 134-7)

In due course Odysseus reached Ithaca, though after losing all his comrades; and recovered his wife and throne.

But the character of Homer's Odysseus, one of the finest in fiction-wise, valiant, compassionate-degenerated in the hands of the Attic dramatists. With them he becomes often a cold Machiavelli; for, not lion. Similarly in Roman writers (who, claiming descent from Troy, tended also to be anti-Greek). From these—particularly from Virgil and Ovid—the tradition passed to Dante, whose *Inferno* (Canto xxvi) punishes the too wily Ulisse among those deceiving counsellors that roast for ever in balls of flame, flitting like fireflies round the Eighth Chasm of Hell. Yet Dante could admire even those that he damned. In a magnificent speech, describing his last voyage, Dante's Ulisse regains his Homeric stature. He tells how from Circe's land, instead of seeking return home, he pushed west past Gibraltar, and thence south-west into the Atlantic; till after five months' sailing, there rose on the horizon the Mount of Purgatory. Then a whirlwind sank him.

> Not fondness for my son, nor piety
> Towards my old father's years, nor yet the claim
> Of love that bade me cheer Penelope,
> Could quell the passion in my heart aflame
> For gathering experience of the world,
> Of human greatness and of human shame.
> (Canto xxvi, 94-9)

Reaching Gibraltar, he urged his aged mariners still onward, into the Atlantic:

> "Brothers," I said, "since ye have reached the West
> Despite a hundred thousand perils run,
> Waste not this little watch that now, at best,
> Is left our eyes and ears, are all be done;
> Lose not the knowledge of that world unknown
> Unpeopled, but pursue the setting sun.
> Consider of what seed ye have been sown,
> Who were not born to waste your days as beasts,
> But to win worth and wisdom for your own."
>
> (112-20)

This imaginative episode seems Dante's own invention. Greekless and so cut off from Homer, he appears ignorant of Odysseus' return home, and of his peaceful death in Ithaca. Latin sources, indeed, could provide the conception of Ulysses as a man of cunning who also navigated far into the West. (By one account he founded Lisbon—"Ulysbona"). Dante may also have been influenced by medieval legends of St. Brandan's voyages; and by the fate of two Genoese explorers lost in the Atlantic about 1291. But, essentially, Dante's version seems Dante's own.

Tennyson draws on both predecessors. Like Homer, he brings Ulysses home to Ithaca (though Homer's Odysseus had returned as sole survivor of his whole fleet). From Homer come also many of Tennyson's most vivid phrases, such as "delight of battle", "windy Troy", "smite the sounding furrows", "baths of all the western stars". But from Dante, not from Homer, comes the old hero's Romantic search for impossible knowledge on this last desperate voyage.

An ancient Greek might have objected: your barbarian poets are too irrational. Your Dante roasts a brave man eternally for a perfectly legitimate ruse of war like the Trojan Horse. Your Tennyson makes him quit his hard-won home, just because he is bored, on a mad quest with a lot of elderly mariners (all really dead years before). A stupid undertaking. He says, 'Death closes all'; yet he hopes to meet the dead Achilles. But Homer's Odysseus had already met the dead Achilles in Hades; and had heard him cry that he would give all his glory to be even the meanest serf among the living. For Homer could face harsh realities. And his Odysseus knew that his first duty was to rule his people. For love of wife, son, and home he had left the beds of two goddesses, and refused even immortality."

It can be answered: "But new poets may change old legends. The voyage is symbolic of Tennyson's rousing himself from impotent melancholy; 'the great Achilles' is symbolic of that Hallam whom Tennyson dreamed of seeing beyond the grave."

True; yet not wholly satisfactory. "Ulysses" remains perhaps a little too rhetorical, too histrionic, too like a *Marseillaise*. It lacks not only the magnificence of the Greek hexameter, but also the simpler dignity, the solider reality, the subtler humanity, of Homer.

Best, no doubt, be thankful for all three poets. Tennyson's "Ulysses", too, has splendid lines. It converted Sir Robert Peel, who had hesitated about Tennyson a pension; it first convinced Carlyle that Tennyson was a "true poet".

And yet, would one find the true Tennyson, better turn perhaps to its companion-piece, printed next it in the Collected Poems—"Tithonus".[1]

For the poet of "The Two Voices" had himself two voices one struggling to be adventurously optimistic; the other, like Virgil, majestic in its sadness—its "immeasurable sadness". And this second voice seems often the deeper and more genuine. "Tithonus" is a lament (like Swift's Struldbrugs in *Gulliver*—but with beauty instead of brutality) for the old, ironic, unalterable tragedy that men crave to live long; and yet, if they live long enough, can only crave to die. Tennyson was never more desolate—nor more inspired.

None the less "Ulysses" gains in force, and feeling, for readers who have grown older. (Strange that it was written by a youth of twenty-four.) For it embodies that courage which refuses to yield to the years—the courage of artists like Titian or Hokusai, never too aged to perfect their art; of writers like Aeschylus, Sophocles, Euripides, Goethe, Hardy, or Tennyson himself, who remained eloquent to the very end; of statesmen like Gladstone, Clemenceau, or Churchill, whose sunsets still kept their ancient fire.[2]

REFERENCES

1. Written about the same period, but not published till 1860, in Thackeray's Cornhill Magazine.
2. Whether or not actually influenced by Tennyson, Baudelaire has produced a curious, Satanic counterpart to "Ulysses" in "Le Vogage" (1859). (The fourth stanza from its end seems a definite echo of Tennyson's "Lotos-Eaters").

9

A Critical Study of Thomas Hardy's Far From the Madding Crowd and the Mayor of Casterbridge

From approximately 1870 to 1890 Hardy was a professional story-teller. He was a literary trouper who designedly set out to earn his living by affording entertainment to a largely indiscriminate public. This is a prime factor and, of all his novels, *Far From the Madding Crowd*, published in 1874, is a good yarn. We can hear its cadences, nostalgically, echoing round venerable malthouses, in Arcadian hayfields, under greenwood trees, now all largely disappeared forever. But in the process of inventing stories, Hardy inevitably encountered greater human issues, as that the human situation often takes on a bigger importance than the tale.

What Hardy is fundamentally concerned with in his novels is the universal predicament of mankind as isolated in a particular tribe. Largely, and specifically in *Far From the Madding Crowd*, he consciously restricts the area of his action and the class of his people. The group he chooses for fictional exploration is a relatively unspoilt community, but it nevertheless carries all the primary vices and weaknesses. The sources of man's badness vary: some of it is inherited even by his chosen people of a pastoral land; some seep insidiously from the world of sophistication and industrial development which is normally situated outside the Wessex boundaries. But whatever the causes, and despite phases of sunny contentedness and exuberant festivity, Hardyan man is basically in a bad way, plaintively lonely in his indifferent circumstances. Life is always a struggle and generally unrosy.

In simple terms, Hardyan existence begins with birth, ends with death, and is perpetually sustained through marriage as established within the context of Victorian Christianity. Throughout all his novels, Hardy is almost pathologically disturbed by the paradox of marriage, especially by the idyllic preliminaries of courtship whose young promise is inevitably tainted by satiric anticipation and by the apparent certitude of post-marital discontent to be sourly endured through make-shift tolerance. In certain novels—*Under the Greenwood Tree*, *The Hand of Ethelberta*, *A Laodicean*, *The Mayor of Casterbridge*, *The Woodlanders*—there is an apparent happy marital ending. But these would seem either twisted or illusory. One of the turbulent centres of *Far From the Madding Crowd* is the squalid disaster of Bathsheba's marriage to Frank Trey: her later compensatory union with Gabriel Oak may satisfy romantic appetites but it does not escape sardonic commentary. Listen to the rustics on the last page of the Book:

> 'Faith,' said Coggan, in a critical tone, turning to his companions, 'the man hev learnt to say "my wife" in a wonderful naterel way, considering how very youthful he is in wedlock as yet—hey, neighbours all?' 'I never heard a skilful old married feller of twenty years' standing pipe "my wife" in a more used note than 'a did,' said Jacob Smallbury. 'It might have been a little more true to nater if 't had been spoke a little chillier, but that wasn't to be expected just now.'
>
> 'That improvement will come wi' time,' said Jan, twirling his eye.

Much of the evil and mischange is centred around the processes of human mating.

The greater blame, in most cases, lies with the woman. It certainly does in the case of Bathsheba Everdene and it may be that personal experiences of the author induced this bias. Such an observation certainly does not mean that Hardy's heroines are not vexatiously charming, nor that, by and large, his chief women characters are not much more vivacious and entertaining than his painfully honest, wooden heroes whose sexual conduct is frustratingly prim and unenterprising. However, before we become too involved with the major characters of *Far From the Madding Crowd*, who for me constitute its most fascinating appeal, in the interests of a total appreciation we must take notice of one or two of the other material features.

A charge of pessimism was early preferred against Hardy, and it still is a popular notion about him today. Hardy persistently deplored the imputation and even as late as February 1922 he wrote in the Apology to *Late Lyrics and Earlier*: what is today, in allusions to the present author's pages, alleged to be "pessimism" is, in truth, only such "questionings" in the exploration of reality, and is the first step towards the soul's betterment, and the body's also. Much depends, I suppose, on one's own interpretation of the word, and any interpretation is bound to be subjective. One reads of the succession of foolish, credulous yet achingly human behaviour on the part of Fanny Ronins, beginning with her seduction and leading through the tawdry agony of her appearance at the wrong church, of her tremulous quest in the snow, of her long trudge in the final throes of pregnancy to a Dorchester Union-house, there to die with Troy's illegitimate child: one notices the grotesque disintegration of Boldwood—a case where a reserved but mannerly farmer, a contentedly placid bachelor, is in a short space of time turned appallingly inside out because of the unthinking antics of a sexual im; a case where there is a gross reversal or order and normalcy and a balanced prosperous man degenerates into a condition of murderous jealousy; one is aware, above all, of the circumstances of Bathsheba's calamitous marriage. Are all these nothing but preposterous shadows cast by a pessimistic mind? Or are they acceptable and genuinely artistic essays to 'explore reality'? Are they proportionately justifiable in a total work where there are many felicitous stretches and where there is a resigned content about much of the country folk's lives? One thing is certain: Herdy was never in danger of underestimating the pressing needs of being.

Often associated with the charge of pessimism is a protest from the smugger critics that there are in Hardy's novels numerous improbabilities, generally governed by misfortune and an over-abundance of coincidence, most often malevolently arranged. Again much depends on one's own assessment of existence and history. Oak's loss of his sheep through the exuberance of a young sheep-dog; the fire in the rick-yard; Bathsheba's choice of seal for the valentine; the ludicrous affair of All Saints' and All Souls' when Sergeant Troy and Fanny Robins waited in different churches; the symbolic stoning of the dog from the Union-house door; Fanny's coffin held up in the mist and Joseph Poorgrass's consequential toping at the Buck's Head; the way, again symbolically, Troy's flowers and bulus were washed from Fanny's grave by the spouting of a malevolent gargoyle: we must again ask, are these incidents defensible set against Hardy's declaration of reality, or are they merely melodramatically impossible. Although the action of any work of fictive prose, the very mechanics of its plot, must in any examination of the total reveal an intrinsic value, I suggest nevertheless that because of Hardy's embracing comprehension of humanity it is unnecessary and unrewarding to quibble over the probabilities of the story line. Hardy would have argued that it is just as likely as not that Oak should lose his sheep, that it is just as likely as not that Fanny's coffin should be delayed. What is far more important in the Hardyan scene, granting faint plausinility to the incident, is the effect of incident on person: the stoicism of Oak in adversity: the hysteria of Bathsheba on opening the coffin and discovering her husband's bastard.

Just as there has been an imbalanced judgement of the so called pessimism and use of ill-chance, so, for the most part, have the Hardyan rustics and their pastoral background been overpraised. Both of course have their place in an overall appreciation, yet a sense of perspective is necessary. Apart from the worthies who form the Mellstock Quire in *Under the Greenwood Tree*, the rustic group in *Far From the Madding Crowd* is probably the most celebrated of Hardy's yokels. There is, however, a derisory implication about this last phrase which Hardy could not accept. The slow-witted, earnest individuals who homed after work and sometimes during it into Warren's Malthouse were neither intellectually gifted nor to the slightest degree educated in the modern sense of the term. But they hold a position in any scheme of wisdom. Their strength lay in what Hardy calls, 'continuity in local history'. What was solid under the seeming bucolic stupidity was a wise tolerance, a largely inarticulate understanding which had accumulated and been handed down the generations where each age had made a rugged and painfully moulded contribution. On to this basic stock was grafted both an individual and communal independence (despite the fact that the people themselves could be bought like cattle at hiring fairs) and a capacity for personally realized pleasure. Out of their limited leisure-time they carved their own entertainment. From the ancient maltster, who was their living historian, down to Joseph Poorgrass, who was congenitally incomplete, they savoured their house of joy with deliberation and seriousness. Their shearin suppers, harvest homes, sheep fairs, and Christmas parties were brief holidays stolen from the year's normal monotony. Yet in *Far From the Madding Crowd*, if not in other places, Hardy shows them happy at their work.

The sexual theme of the novel (which despite all the other attributes is the heart of the novel) is one woman's relations with three men. Three of these protagonists are country people removed from the rustic group only by degrees of refinement: the fourth is an intruder from an alien world whose values are not the values of the rural earth. Bathsheba Everdone stands at the centre of all the emotional disturbance. Attractive and flirtatious, she is sometimes uncertain of her sex's power but is generally prepared to exploit it: she is one of the most enigmatic of Hardy's heroines—nothing so paradoxically fickle as Elfride Swancourt yet never earning the compassion that Tess does. But she does win our respect and affection as she struggles through dilemmas largely of her own making. On the periphery of her heart the male contestants pursue their sexual destinies according to their widely differing natures. Troy, the first to win her, does so uninhibitedly, sensually and selfishly—He is the extra-rural 'know-all', and the country girls have never really met anything like him—yet in his overthrow, in the kinds of his personality, we can discern grim twists which are an integral part of the human scene. In his thwarting of the second suitor, Boldwood, we feel there is something biologically right: it would have been an insult to youth and beauty for Bathsheba to have become Mrs. Boldwood; yet in the person of Boldwood, perhaps better than anywhere else except in the person of Tess, Hardy drapes the ordinary and dull with the harsh splendours of tragedy and elevates them with the dignity of suffering. Oauisa moon-faced, rugged, sheep-hearted farmer of high moral conservat'sm. Many people consider this heroic Hodge to be the agricultural image of Victorian integrity. He is a good man, like Giles Winterborne, and very reassuring to have around in a crisis, as Bathsheba discovered on a number of occasions until she finally decided to have him around permanently. And so it well ends happily with the traditional wedding.

Far From the Madding Crowd was one of Hardy's early novels. It was hailed by the public and set him on the road to commercial success. Yet for all its being a sheep and shepherd novel, and without committing ourselves to the controversies of pessimism and malicious coincidence, we can perhaps see in it symptoms of dark analyses to come, when Hardy was to probe deeper into the human soul and situation.

Even in this modern age when mechanized pleasure-seekers throng through Dorchester heading for the Dorset and Devon coasts, you can, of a summer's evening, walk round the old city boundaries which have been charmingly and ingeniously preserved for identification by rows of tall trees, and you can imagine yourself, without too much difficulty, back in Mayor Henchard's town, the Casterbridge of Hardyan myth. Although many of the original buildings have been replaced, you can readily identify a number of places which constitute the setting for *The Mayor of Casterbridge*. On the outskirts of the old town but well within the new you can discover, unspoilt and well-tended, Maumbury Ring, the Roman amphitheatre where Henchard arranged to meet Susan Newson on her return to his care; in Durngate Street there are vestiges of Lucetta's house, 'High Place Hall' : Mill Lane is the original for 'Mixen Lane' where 'vice ran freely in and out of certain doors'; in the West Walk you can trace the spot where Farfrae organized his improvised dance after Henchard's plans for celebration had ignominiously collapsed ; and down on the London Road you can recognize the two bridges over the From which figure so symbolically in the novel. Just out of the town is Max Gate, Hardy's celebrated house which he was building at the same time as he was writing *The Mayor of Casterbridge*. Significantly, he was living in Dorchester at the time.

Dorchester has a central geographical importance in Hardy's Wessex; besides in *The Mayor*, it figures in many novels stories and poems—most often, of course, under the name of *Casterbridge* : it is essentially *a country* town as Newson's daughter observed as she entered it for the first time :

> 'What an old-fashioned place it seems to be,' 'said Elizabeth-Jane, while her silent mother mused on other things than topography. 'It is huddled all together and it is shut in by a square wall of trees, like a plot of garden ground by a box edging'.
>
> Its squareness was, indeed, the characteristic which most struck the eye in this antiquated borough of Casterbridge —at that time, recent as it was, untouched by the faintest sprinkle of modernism. It was compact as a box of dominoes. It had no suburbs in the ordinary sense. Country and town met at a mathematical line.

This is of course only one of many descriptions in the novel of a whole or part of the town,architecturally, spiritually historically it has dominating and brooding functions in the book, but perhaps one of its most important implications is to be found in the above passage. It is a 'huddled together' urban centre, a focus for all the rural acres about it which themselves vary from the desolate and lonely to the fertile and lush. But it is not urban in the sense that industrial cities are urban; it is set in a sea of country parishes and its heart is a country heart and its business country business; it 'was the complement of the rural life around; not its urban opposite. Bees and butterflies in the cornfields, at the top of the town, who desired to get to the meads at the bottom, took no circuitous course, but flew straight down High Street without wany apparent consciousness that they were traversing strange latitudes.' But, and one must make this qualification country purity gets tarnished by apparently the simple fact of urbanness. Casterbridge faults are perhaps not so vicious as those of the smoky cities to the east and north but there is a certain deterioration in standards among its inhabitants which is not confined to the prostitutes of Mixen Lane nor to the topers in Peter's Finger. Solomon Longways, Christophers Coney, Mother Cuxsom and company are a harder lot than Bathsheba's labourers; they have lost their country innocence; peasant wisdom has turned into peasant cunning ; by living together in a town, no matter how small and countrified, much of the magic has rubbed off.

Such refashioning of the rustics may not be a 'step towards the soul's betterment' but it is indubitably a subtler and maturer 'exploration of reality'. But then, of course, *The Mayor of Casterbridge*, published in 1886, is a much maturer novel than *Far From the Madding Crowd.* Just as its situational complex is dominated by the town of Casterbridge, so are all its characters subsidiary to the lonely power of Michael Henchard. Hardy never created a male character like him before or afterwards. He is not in the tradition of heroic do-gooders such as Springrove, Smith, Oak, Yeobright. He has been compared with Lear but such a forced parallel is, I think, a ludicrous notion either over-elaborate or lamentably unthought out ; the tragic circumstances of the two, both inwardly in the matter of spiritual conflict and outwardly the matter of malevolent entanglement, are so vastly different. Henchard has been represented as a protagonist in the perennial battle of the generations, with Farfrae representing the younger and pushful age. Besides the fact of Farfrae being pallid beside him, I submit that Henchard, peculiarly, represents all generations. He has that brutish obstinacy which is indispensable to the top bull in the herd, that one-tracked masterfulness which is an essential mark of a leader (it does not matter a leader of what or whom—leadership is a cardinal quality irrespective of the size of the pool); he possesses drive and energy and for a period of twenty years the arrangements of furtune were disposed benevolently in his favour.

There are, nevertheless, tragic (I use the epithet advisedly) emptinesses in his personality. There was in the first place a rejection of human affection (the sale of his wife and child in the furmity booth was, it is true, largely unintentional, but was nevertheless part of the tragic handicap which marked all his being and doing). Like many self-made men of domineering temperament he found that he could not do without love; but in Henchard's case it needed to be of a particular kind. The anaemic wifeliness of Susan was unsatisfactory—not, oddly enough, for his red blood but for his special need; the sexual toying with Lucetta temporarily filled a want but very inadequately. It came to dawn on Henchard that what his frustrated being craved for was the love of a young daughter; and even when Elizabeth-Jane proved ironically to be no daughter of his, he still bitterly demanded her affection.

I referred in the first essay to charges against Hardy of pessimism and of his overdoing the incidence of mischance. This mood and factor are even more grimly in evidence in *The Mayor of Casterbridge*. Some of us may consider it irrationally outrageous that for Henchard things should prosper so extraordinarily well for twenty years and collapse so calamitously in two. The price, we may think, is exorbitant for a drunken sin. To my mind, however, Michael Henchard was not punished for selling his wife; he was punished because he was himself, and the selling of his wife was part of his punishment.

The crucial feature of Henchard's personality was that, like the lemmings, he possessed a compulsive propensity for self-destruction. He was not a man who could subtly adapt or exploit adversity; he attempted, through contemptuous and brute force, to rearrange the pattern of circumstances, only to experience that this way things become even more inimical ; yet in his wrong-doing and his blundering, no judgement of others was more bitter than his own self-recrimination.

Although I have largely rejected the symbolic interpretation of Farfrae and the younger generation, it must be admitted that the mere fact of Farfrae's existence and his irreproachable, well-intentioned conduct constituted paradoxically the hard core of malevolence against which Henchard uncompromisingly banged his head. Henchard discovered a gruff affection for Farfrae in the first place and pleaded with him—very much counter to the young Scot's plan and inclination to remain with him in Casterbridge. It was with reluctance that Farfrae took his place in a doomed web of human relationship and incompatibility; with reluctance he captured, appallingly swiftly, Henchard's prestige and possessions—his business, his house, his mayor's office, his mistress and finally, the savagest thing of all, the girl that Henchard perversely and irrationally considered to be his daughter. However he may have been angered and exasperated, we must feel for the 'fangless lion' in this emotional predicament. He shifts from indignity to ignobility in an effort to retain Elizabeth-Jane and this conclusive phase surely holds the tragic crux of the matter; it is a time, too, when we feel genuinely an unqualified compassion. As we see him lie to Newson; as he conjures with an idea of betraying the secret of Elizabeth-Jane's birth to Farfrae to prevent their marriage; as we observe him, once more reduced to the level of haytrusser, examining with furtive sentiment an old glove, a cast-off shoe, a scrap of her handwriting; when we watch this man of erstwhile self-sufficiency buying a cage and a gold-finch for a wedding present; when we read the first clause of his mordant weil—'That Elizabeth-Jane Farfrae be not told of my death, or made to grieve on account of me'—it is on these occasions we squirm with embarrassing knowledge of human vicissitude and ache for all the unloved.

To such is power and ambition reduced but in the degeneration there is ignited a certain human splendour. Henchard dies without compromise; terribly wounded in heart but scorning, in the grand manner, compassion and patronage, and maintaining that searingly lonely but magnificent isolation of soul and independence of spirit.

10

Heroes of Graham Greene

Mustafa Mond says to the Savage in Aldous Huxley's *Brave New World* : '. . . . Civilization has absolutely no need of nobility or heroism.' Thank God we have not arrived at that state of affairs but, curiously enough, the hero has still disappeared from the major fiction of the West. Since the reaction against romanticism in the later 19th century a '*fallen democrat*' or a 'struggling bourgeois' has been elbowing him out. His displacement has been compeleted by a number of social, economic and political factors. In Graham Greene, as in most contemporary novelists, we have what may be called an anti-hero. In place of a glamorous character we have an unimpressive, even drab human being. We are not overwhelmed by him, but we cannot be indifferent to him either. Cast in our own mould he does call forth certain reactions in us. In fact by being closer to essential humanity he engages our emotions more effectively than a romantic and extraordinary personage is like to do who comes from on high only to dazzle and startle us.

Greene takes even an average man a peg or two down. Some of his memorable characters are sinners and wicked men. Other novelists before him have been attracted towards them. Dickens, for example, was interested in exploring the fascinating possibilities of evil. Other Victorian novelists like

Thackeray, George Eliot have described how a man or woman made some unfortunate mistake and was enmeshed in the coils of circumstances. Meredith, Conrad and Hardy give us heroes broken and for ever disillusioned. Life is not a series of triumphs, each stage being an advance on the preceding one. Bunyan's Christian belongs to the realm of fable and allegory. A stricter measure of truth is demanded of the modern novelist. Greene goes farthest in this respect. He puts in the centre persons who do some wrong or commit some sin not by accident but as a result of deliberate choice, knowing full well what its consequences would be, adding a new dimension to the realistic novel.

Pinkie in *Brighton Rock* is a teenager inordinately given to a life of crime and evil. He arrogates to himself the powers of a little despot over his clique. He has several cold-blooded murders to his credit. We can see his razor flashing in the dark and mercilessly slashing somebody. He successfully keeps on dodging the authorities and taking it out on them, as it were, by yet another crime. With the prostitute Ida trying to track him down he can think of no other device for saving his skin except marrying the slum girl Rose. Scobie in *The Heart of the Matter* is the chief of police in a British West African district who should keep strict vigilance over diamond-smugglers rather than himself appear to be an accomplice of one of them. His wife being away in the Cape Colony he lives in sin with Mrs. Holt. Though a Catholic, he takes the communion without receiving absolution as he would not promise to give up adultery. Father Monte in *The Power and the Glory* is nicknamed the Whisky priest and anything can be coaxed out of him by offering him a drink. He has fathered a child by a woman living in an inland village. When the priests are exterminated and hounded out of a certain Mexican state this fugitive clerk stays behind, not because he has any desire to be a martyr but just because he is too craven-hearted to risk coming out in the open. He never scruples to go in for contraband liquor in the midst of his official duties—administering the sacraments and saying masses.

His heroes, no doubt, show up the seamy side of life. A quotation from Cardinal Newman, in *The Lawless Roads* describes human life as a 'vision to dizzy and appal.' That may well serve as key to Greene's own delineation of life. Betrayal, cruelty, distrust, animosity, deception are the elements of which this life is compounded and his central characters have their full quota of vice and evil.

There is, however, something in a typical Greene character which raises him to the heights of heroism. A persistent feeling on his part of not having been able to live up to a certain ideal is what distinguished him from the fun-of-the mill stuff. This causes misery and suffering and qualms of conscience. Pinkie is perhaps his hero forthest gone towards damnation and even he shudders to think of death without contrition. Dying a sudden death is something he can hardly reconcile himself to. He recalls a sentence to fortify himself with : 'Between the stirrup and the ground he sought something found.' An acute and agonising sense of personal guilt drives Scobie to desperation. He blames everything sadly going awry on himself, whether it is his being superseded or his wife being shunned by British families for her love of poetry. The climate of the place, the growing uncongeniality of his job and everything else which can even remotely account for their married life being a failure he takes upon himself. It presses heavily on his mind that his conduct does not conform to the doctrine of the Catholic Church. Out of sheer timidity he can't face up to the facts of life. His soul is in great turmoil of disquietude and unhappiness. The priest has a painful realisation of how far he has fallen from grace, how a poor representative he is of the church, how unworthy of the holy office he holds. All his heroes are involved in a fierce conflict, both external and internal. They can evade the long arm of the law but it is not possible for them to avoid the persecution of God through their own conscience. His heroes writhe in inward agony and have been compared to El Greco's paintings, twisted and distorted and tormented. This tendency of the novelist can best be appreciated in the light of a remark in his travel book *Journal Without Maps*: 'Like a revelation, when I was fourteen I realised the pleasure of cruelty. I wasn't interested any longer in walks on commons, in playing cricket on the beach. It was as if I had discovered that the way to enjoy life was to appreciate pain'. Needless to say the torment to which Greene subjects his hero is comparable to that of the tragic hero.

His protagonists look like disciples and yet they are truly aware of the transcendental power of God. The priest in *The Potting Shed* boastfully asserts that there isn't a drop of faith anyone can squeeze out of his saying Mass and performing other rituals of the Church. He was once a great believer and it was his prayers through which the life of his nephew was saved. And he had declared to God that since I have nothing of greater value to offer you, take away my faith and give me James' life. This actually happened. The boy who was given up for dead came back to life. One couldn't believe in a god one could understand. James further says that his uncle lives not in a room without faith, but in a room from which faith has gone, which is quite a different matter. A man's faith in God is proved by his ever-recurring doubt. One who knows God knows less of Him than one who doubts Him. The hero in Greene's novel makes a strenuous effort to encompass faith in an apparently godless universe. By every act of transgression he provokes the Wrath of God till at the end he has a dreadful impression that damnation is closing in on him. But it should be remembered that despair and anguish are the badge of every aspiring soul. Only the smug and the indifferent are immune from them. As Scobie puts it: 'only the man of good will carries always in his heart this capacity for damnation.'

Green does nothing to make his heroes look big. As time passes and as experience accumulates their humility and weakness come out into vivid relief. They represent failure, frustration, isolation and gloom. His sinners and failures and rotters hold themselves—and only themselves—answerable for allowing their low passions to subdue their higher self. Anthony Farrant in *England Made Me* is ever and even troubled by the glimmerings of an old code of conduct according to which it is shameful for him to live on the mercy of millionaire who has kept his sister as his mistress. The memories of his forefathers stir up in him and hinder his adjustment. Minty, the journalist, is another outcast. The novelist's comment is 'they had't the resources to hold their place, but the world had so conditioned them that 'they hadn't the vigour to resist. They were not fresh enough, optimistic enough. . . . .' Over against them we have krough. It is another name for the ruthless impersonality of international finance. He has built up his prosperity on the skill with which he can perpetrate a fraud and control the trends of the market. Lies and frame-ups are unabashedly used to get inconvenient people out of his way. This unscrupulous, figure-happy capitalist is a veritable monster. Even a minor character Fred Hall has a gay and wonderful time, being assured of a continued supply of cigarettes and drinks by his master. It may almost be taken for a rule in Greene, that those who are worried and distressed and inwardly agitated are by common standards sinners and criminals, but they are moving on to a higher destiny. In contrast with them there are those who look very well pleased with themselves and the world, gliding smoothly on the surface, seldom behaving indecorously; but they are the ones in whom the moral fibre has decayed and all the fine faculties are atrophied and whose vision does not extend beyond 'Here' and 'Now'. Benedrix in *The End of the Affair*, Minty, the slum girl Rose, the unhappy police superintendent in *Its A Battlefield*, Raven in *A Gun For Sale* are all people who are perishing whereas those having surface existence are flourishing.

But they will not utterly perish; at least Greene gives us this assurance. They will not be struck down in the end like the heroes of Sophocles. The way God's mercy operates is incomprehensible.Here is a colloquy between Father Rank and Mrs. Scobie :

"For goodness sake, Mrs. Scobie, don't imagine you—— or I——know a thing about God's mercy."

"The Church says. . . ."

"I know what the Church says. The Church knows all the rules.

But it doesn't know what goes on in a single human heart. . . ."

He loved God. Even Pinkie, the least lidable character, can look forward to salvation, though his deeds would give him out to be demned, it there ever was one. Rose does not ask for absolution. She would be rather like him—demand. 'She would have formed the courage now to kill herself if she hadn't been afraid that somewhere in that obscure country-side of death they might miss each other—mercy operating somehow for one and not for the other.'

Fault has been found not so much with his heroes as with the view of life which they present, and which, it can he safely inferred, is Greene's own view. Arnold Kettle, for instance, has strongly protested against too dismal a view of human life that Greene reinforces through his key characters. Kettle's chief objection is that Greene makes life seem more sordid than it really is. Another critic, Graham Martin, is unhappy because Greene jumps from a highly specialised situation to a universal vision. What, for example, is the rationale for introducing such lines as these: 'Nobody here could ever talk about a heaven on earth. Heaven remained rigidly in its proper place on the other side of death, and on this side flourished the injustices, the cruelties, the meanness that elsewhere people so cleverly hushed up. Here you could love human beings nearly as God loved them, knowing the worst. . . .'[1] Or take this from the same novel: 'Point me out the happy man and I will point you out eitnc ɾegotism, selfishness, evil—or an absolute ignorance.

Outside the rest house he stopped again. The lights inside would have given an extraordinary impression of peace if one hadn't known just as the stars on this clear night gave also an impression of remoteness, security, freedom. If one knew, he wondered, the facts, would one have to feel pity even for the planets? If one reached what they called the heart of the matter?

It may he taken as part of his novelistic technique to set forth his own 'philosophy' and establish his own attitudes by stating clearly and emphatically the response of his heroes and other key characters to a situation and thus effectively ruling out any protest or dissent. If E.M. Forster, Aldous Huxley, T.S. Eliot and other sensitive spirits of the age bring a serious indictment against the civilization and institutions that we have built up there must be something the matter. The amazing unanimity in their reactions can't just be put down to fortuitous chance.

It is not a little surprising that Greene can enlist our sympathy and compassion for his hero in spirit of his mounting crimes and glaring weaknesses. This he does by first placing him in an absolutely realistic framework. 'Seediness' can truly be called his forte. Then he often brings in certain extonuating circumstances. Modern Psychology has diminished, if not destroyed, the villainy of the villain. We can never escape the question : why is Pinkie what he is? Greene will take all possible pains to tell us, of course in an apparently casual tone, what his upbringing has been like. Had he not received a traumatic vision of the universal violence in his childhood? Understandably enough, heaven to him was a word : hell was something he could trust. Scobie, himself a friendless and lonely man, could not withhold his pity for Mrs. Holt, whose husband was killed on board the torpedoed ship within a few days of their marriage. He damned his soul first by taking communion without confession because he hated upsetting his wife by a disclosure of adulterous life and next by committing suicide as it would have been unbearable for him to cause pain to either his wife or Mrs. Holt. Even in the last act, that is of committing suicide he is awfully concerned with the question of his wife getting the insurance money. So he feigns angina and takes an overdose of evipan and in order that his deliberately planned suicide may be taken as the result of his carelessness goes on jotting down regularly in his diary about the changing condition of his heart. Anthony and Minty, rooted as they were to a code of conduct different from that of the successful people of the world, found themselves square pegs in round holes. The priest, at no small risk to himself, carries on quietly and unobtrusively the work of the church. If the last rites are to be performed, no matter to whom and where, the priest would throw all caution to the winds and go right away, timid though by nature he is. Greene's heroes are not confined to right and wrong matters of current ethical beliefs : they are fighting their lone battle between good and evil. And if their choice is ultimately for the good we cannot doubt the mysterious mercy of God for them and the spiritual deserts awaiting them.

Though in a sense his heroes are used as a vehicle for depicting life's horror and sterility, in another sense they also reveal *the power and the glory that shines through them*. In their fallings away and strayings the dread of damnation relentlessly follows them. Greene seems to be arguing in effect that they with their misery and suffering are far closer to God than those who live in appearances, subscribing glibly to current beliefs and dogma. May be this is an encroachment of Greene's catholic faith on his art. But we do have a feeling that those whom the world calls sinners and who are apparently at fault but in whom the divine spark is not absolutely extinguished, need not despair of God's mercy at the end. Of course we may not feel comfortable and happy with the picture of human life that he gives us, there is no getting away from the harsh reality contained in it. The priest's last act before his execution is to give absolution to an American gangster. May we not reasonably hope that God's fund of forgiveness and compassion will be found fuller than his creature's. Some of us may not like this intrusion of God and His dispensation in our common scheme of life but it should be remember that his heroes are invariably tormented by supramundane concerns in moments of stress. Greene's hero is a symbol of the modern man going down in the struggle of life, suffering grave spiritual crisis, constantly brooding over his lapses, the damned has that he has made of his life, following in the footsteps of Satan and yet, to his infinite wonder perhaps finding himself knocking at the doors of God. Through his heroes Greene links the petty affairs of the humdrum would with such questions of perennial interests as God and the nature of existence. His heroes act as a bridge between the topical and the universal.

REFERENCE

1. *The Heart of the Matter*, p. 34.

11

Bernard Shaw: Saint Joan

It is natural to wonder why Bernard Shaw chose Saint Joan as a subject for a play and then worked on it with a fascinated devotion in the years 1922 and 1923. He had been tired after completing *Back to Methuselah*, the five separate pieces which made up what he called his 'Metabiological Pentateuch'. In that work he had surveyed the span of human life and considered the necessity and the ability to prolong it in order to gain further wisdom. His scrutiny and conjecture extended from the Garden of Eden to the world of thirty thousand years ahead of us. He had outlined and in his Preface had explained his own religion of Creative Evolution. He could have felt that he had spoken his mind sufficiently on what H.G. Wells called 'First and Last Things'. He might have been expected to turn back to the problems and humours of the contemporary scene and to use the stage once more for his constant stimulation of the public and private mind and conscience in the affairs of here and now. This indeed he continued to do with undiminished wit and vitality when he had got another play about religion off his chest.

How then did the Main of Orleans find her way into the mind of Shaw and, one might fairly and, into his heart as well ? His sympathies were deeply engaged, but his sense of proportion, not always conspicuous in his praise or indictment of policies and people in our time, was conspicuously maintained on this occasion. Joan's fight for freedom in her faith would of course stir his compassion. But her powerful opponents who convicted her of heresy, sorcery, and witchcraft are given in the play a cleverly reasoned and eloquent defence, at least in the matter of religious deviation. The allegations of sorcery and witchcraft were nonsensical. The English Commander in France, the Earl of Warwick, is also allowed to state ably and fairly his fear that the political heresy implicit in Joan's actions would endanger the whole structuıe of medieval society; to him she was an enemy in the field of government. This was accidental because she was not in any way a student of affairs of state. None the less she could be regarded as a menace to the feudal order from which Warwick derived wealth and power.

Shaw's fair play for all sides was carried so far that instead of running into serious trouble with the members of the Roman Catholic Church he was attacked by some of its opponents, scholars who had closely studied the history of Joan's Trial. They protested that Shaw's claim for the legality of the proceedings according to the ecclesiastical code of the time was unjustified. But that is not a matter on which the average play-goer or reader is capable of judging.

In St. John Ervine's ample and excellent life of Shaw it is explained that the idea of play about Saint Joan was first put to him by his friend Sir Sydney Cockerell, Curator of the Fitzwilliam Museum at Cambridge. Then Mrs. Shaw, who liked the project, resolved to encourage it. She knew that she might provoke Shaw's resistance if the idea was too strongly or insistently urged. So she quietly left books on the Maid lying about for him to see. Her tact had its desired result. Gradually Shaw was interested, attracted, and finally involved.

The subject, as Mrs. Shaw knew, could knew, well be congenial. Shaw was always interested in religion. When he was once asked if he was an atheist he replied that he had no use for a negative creed or an evasive philosophy. He admired positive views, brisk action and audacity. Among the characters in his historical plays had been famous conquerors,

Napoleon, Julius Caesar, and, in another way, Cleopatra. The essence of Joan's character as he saw it lay not only in her simplicity, her innocence, and her ignorance of the world's guile but in her assurance, energy, boundless courage, and capacity for quick decision. She was never handicapped by the habit of thinking and re-thinking her military tactics or her relations with God. Believing herself to be led forth and guided onward by her Saints and her Voices which came direct to her from heaven she radiated confidence and so put self-confidence in others, especially in the defeated and discouraged leaders and soldiers of the French forces.

She was not to be over-awed by people owning titles or dressed in authority. In this too she appealed to Shaw as he planned his play. There is frequently a paradox in the characters and conduct of Socialists and not least of Shaw himself. Their policy hands immense powers to the State and its administrative officials while it seeks to end private exploitation. Yet Socialists are instinctively freedom-loving people, usually the first to insist on personal rights and liberties and swift to challenge the use or abuse of the law by those entitled to impose the discipline without which their policies are impossible. The dramatist himself was always in revolt against accepted ideas and conventional moralities. Inside Shaw the theoretical Socialist was Shaw the practising anarchist, crying out and struggling to get out. He had welcomed the plays of Ibsen, who was no Socialist, because they exposed the shams and tyrannies of bourgeois society in Norway and by implication all over the world. The Ibsenite hero was 'the alone-standing man'. In the Maid of Orleans could be discovered 'the alone-standing woman'. Here was a theme which Shaw could relish and one that he steadily developed as he traced his heroine's course from the farm in Lorraine to the terrible death in Rouen.

The first scene, set in a seigneurial castle between the territories of Lorraine and Champagne, might have been described by Polonius as pastoral-comical. A milord is cursing his steward because the hens will not lay. Into his presence Joan, a farmer's daughter still well under twenty, forces her way. Her first words are as significant as they are short. 'God morning, captain squire. Captain, you are to give me a horse and armor and some soldiers and send me to the Dauphin. These are your orders from my Lord.'

(Incidentally, the spelling of armor was Shaw's constant preference in words of this kind. He argued that the English honour, labour, and so on had come from the Latin honor and labour by way of the French whose interpolated 'u' was unnecessary. He had reason, as well as American usage, on his side. But so strong is English conservatism in matters of orthography that even the political party which might be expected to welcome a sensible reform prefers the Labour to the Shavian Labor. Yet the English practice is absurdly inconsistent; when the relevant adjectives are employed they write laborious and mix honorary with honourable.)

Joan's words immediately reveal her character and declare her purpose. She is curt with her social superiors, but not discourteous. She announces her need and her aim without hesitation and without a syllable wasted. She is sure that she is under God's orders, thus intimating her belief that God will be in command when she is a commander in the field. Soon she makes plain the source of her authority. She has talked with St. Catharine and St. Margaret. For her there are these Voices in the air. 'The Voices,' 'says the Squire, 'come from your imagination'. 'Of course', answers Joan, 'that is how the messages of God come to us'. Shaw has given her a reply which it is difficult to counter.

The early pastoral-comical episode makes an extremely skilful opening for the historical-heroical-tragical play which is to follow. The audience has been lightly and amusingly introduced to the tremendous chain of events. In flash the hard core of the country-girl's character has been established. The first actress to play Joan in England was Sybil Thorndike who emphasized the rural quality and sturdy quality of one who had come from the farm and would gladly return to it, if she survived, when her appointed task had been completed. This Maid was enjoying herself as she cheerfully told her betters what she could and would do if she got only a fraction of a chance.

Since that first night in 1924 many of England's leading actresses and many more across the world have played the part. Some have been slight in physique and carried on to the stage the look of a frail and almost unearthly creature, so winning pathos. It must be remembered that Shaw selected Sybil Thorndike for the role; he had in mind a working woman of the land who would mix easily with the troops and find the management of a horse a natural exercise, a soldier first and a saint to be.

'Nothing can save our side now but a miracle', says one of the despairing landed gentry. He adds that he finds the girl to be something of a miracle herself. Joan gets her way and is given her military chance. Then a minor miracle does happen. The steward rushes in to say 'The hens are laying like mad. Five dozen eggs!' So the thought may arise that this queer, compelling girl, so potent among poultry, may be able to work wonders among men.

In the second scene the play moves swiftly forward. Joan has now become a soldier and she is irrepressible. She has reached the royal throne-room. In the earlier episode Shaw makes her speak in the ordinary language that an educated person might use, but now she talks ungrammatically. 'Be that Dauphin ?' 'Be that Queen ?' she asks as she is brought before royalty. The object presumably is to emphasize her rusticity but it is odd that she was less of the peasant in her speech when she was only starting on her way up.

Her purpose is to rouse the Dauphin to action. He must be crowned. He must take command. To enliven and encourage him is not easy since he is a nervous little creature who hates war and only wants a quiet life. Since he is quick-witted there is still good comedy in the play; his interchanges with the fatuous Chamberlain and the shrewd Archbishop are lively and entertaining. The rumour that Joan can perform miracles impels them to test her. Will she recognize the Dauphin who has hidden himself ? She quickly discovers him and then at once animates him with a new spirit. He had feared the nuisance and responsibility of being crowned. Now, with Joan beside him, he is ready for the ceremony. But he will be no general. Joan will lead the army to raise the siege of Orleans. The Dauphin's change is not miraculous, but in its way it is wonderful.

Another minor miracle occurs in the third scene set on the banks of the river Loire. In order to avoid a heavily guarded bridge it is necessary for the French to get across by rafts and so take the English in the rear. They cannot get up-stream with the current and the wind against them. But what if a strong wind should suddenly blow in the right quarter ? In answer to Joan's prayers the wind instantly changes. Of course both the flood of eggs, the identification of the Dauphin, and the sudden change of weather could be happy accidents. Shaw could have told his story without them. But he was not a rationalist who discounted anything of a miraculous kind. In his long and illuminating Preface to another religious play, *Androcles and the Lion*, he had discussed the Gospel accounts of the miracles of Christ which some find fatal to belief. 'Get rid of the miracles', Rousseau had said, 'and the whole world will fall at the feet of Jesus Christ.' Shaw strongly disagreed. 'The intellectual energies of sceptics and divines', he wrote, 'have been wasted for generations in arguing about the miracles on the assumption that Christianity is at stake in the controversy.'

Shaw accepted that apparent miracles might naturally occur through faith-healing. They were irrelevant, he insisted, to the validity of the Christian message which, as a Socialist, he thought to be a moral and even economic one. He included in his play the little wonderments of the Joan chronicles and legends because they belonged to their time and its credulities. But what matters for him was the high purpose of her mission and the valour of her spirit. If her Voices are dismissed as imagined they might none the less be valid. He knew that seeing visions and hearing strange communications have been the experience of many remarkable people whose wisdom posterity has approved though they were regarded as crazy at the time. (William Blake is a case in point). The Church which included witch-craft in its charges against the wonder-working Joan had to cononize her in the end.

In Scene Four, set in the Earl of Warwick's tent in the English camp, Joan does not appear in person. This shows the play-wright's awareness of theatrical necessities. Her part is very long and exacting and the actress must have a break. The chaplain Stogumber, John Bull in a cassock, continues to let laughter break in since he is a favourite type of Shavian butt and almost a clown, the crass patriot who must vehemently assert that the English are never wrong. But here in the corridors of power there is not only comedy. We are led on to grave issues of religion and politics. Warwick realizes that something new may be stirring in his feudal world and in Europe where nationality was a concept scarcely understood. There was then no unified France but a series of French provinces with contending rulers deeply divided. The Burgundians, for example, were on England's side. What Joan was creating by instinct and not by deliberate plan was the image of a single France united under the Crown.

To Cauchon, Bishop of Beauvais, this is intolerable. 'Call this side of her heresy Nationalism if you will', he says. 'I can find no better name for it. I can only tell you that it is essentially anti-Catholic and anti-Christian, for the Catholic Church knows only one realm and that is the realm of Christ's kingdom. Divide that kingdom into nations and you dethrone Christ'.

That is a very significant excerpt from a dialogue between Warwick and Cauchon which is vital to the understanding of the play. Cauchon wants France divided for religious reasons and Warwick, for reasons of privilege, wants power in England divided between the great land-owners whom he represents. A king may be tolerated as a figure-head, but he is not to interfere with clerical and baronial dominion. Joan, with her individualism, her royalism, and her nationalism, is a menace to them both. 'It goes deep, my lord', says Warwick to the Bishop. 'It is the protest of the individual soul against the interference of priest or peer.' Then he adds 'I should call it Protestantism if I had to find a name for it.'

It is thus made plain what peril lies ahead of Joan and these are made still more apparent in the fifth scene. Success has made her less, not more, secure. Because of it she could be sold to Warwick by a traitor in her camp for a large sum. Her victories are her danger because they cause the jealousy of those who had lost battles before she won them. The brave and friendly soldier Dunois admires and befriends her, but he knows that if she has one failure in the field there will be no mercy. To the clerics she is a damnable heretic because of her claim to talk directly with God through her Voices instead of through the orthodox channels of the Church. 'You stand alone', says the Archbishop, 'utterly alone', and Dunois confirms it. 'That is the truth', he adds. 'Head it.'

The way to the great Trial Scene has been amply prepared. Has there been too much ? Warwick's speeches about political power may have seemed irrelevant to those thinking only in terms of Joan's personal tragedy, but they were necessary to show the cohesion of the enmities into which Joan has unwittingly wandered. The play drives most poignantly a tour compassion because it exhibits the final agony and destruction of a solitary girl. But Shaw as a political dramatist was no less concerned to exhibit the social forces which were standing over and soon to crush 'the alone-standing woman'.

The sixth scene is long but few would care to miss a word of it. Traxials are always 'good theatre'. There is every kind of dramatic conflict. The legally minded ecclesiastics know that the heresy is all that matters but they have to quell the spasms of hatred and the blood-lust of those on their side who will harp so pettily on the alleged witch-craft. The Inquisitor has to clear the air with his logic and does so in a lengthy monologue which takes the actor seven or eight minutes to deliver. Yet, if it be well spoken, a theatrical audience is always held by every word of it.

The tension is kept steadily mounting. There is the growing horror of threatened torture and of a certain conviction, then Joan's admission of heresy which averts the death-sentence only to be followed by the condemnation to life-imprisonment. This evokes Joan's heart-rending speech about the freedom of the air and of the hills which she will never abandon. Here is Shaw's word-mastery at its simplest and strongest. She prefers the stake to the cell and goes to the flames. Then comes a brilliant touch. Stogumber, who has clamoured for the fire, breaks down completely when he sees its reality; his sudden humanity is in moving contrast with the inhuman proceedings. The last line comes from Warwick and how pregnant it is! When the Executioner tells him that he has seen the last of Joan he says 'The last of her? H'm. I wonder'.

It has been argued that the play should end there, that it is more than long enough, and that the Epilogue with its mingled parade of ghosts and characters still living in 1456 is a mistake. It is a sequel and surely a necessary sequel to that uneasy remark made by Warwick. After a quarter of century the Maid has been 'rehabilitated after a fashion', as Shaw put it. The ironies of that are pointed with forcible strokes. The King has learned the way of the fickle world and says that if she returned to life she would be burned again in six months. Sadder still, Joan knows that the victory of any cause may be the loss of it. 'Woe unto me when all men praise me', she says. That was a thought always in Shaw's mind. He had known the cost of conquest.

He had first used the stage as a platform for the unpopular ideas in which he believed and for a long time the result was far from popular. Then he became successful, approved, applauded, and enriched. But he was no longer listened to as a rebel and prophet. What drew the larger audiences was the lively and enjoyable entertainment which he provided. He realized that his cherished opinions were less understood and absorbed by the many thousands who now laughed and clapped than by the faithful few of the old days when his audiences had been very small but anxious for the doctrine. When Joan was honoured far and wide and worshipped as a Saint in heaven who would remember the Maid of Arc, standing alone among the great ones who destroyed her? There lay the essential Joan. The Epilogue drives home the point effectively.

After 'rehabilitation' four-and-a-half centuries passed. Then Joan was designated Venerable in 1904, declared Bleassed in 1908, and canonized in 1920. Three years later came Shaw's play, produced first in New Yourk in 1923, in London in 1924, and thereafter in translations on many stages of the world. The general truth of Shaw's version of Joan's story in what he described as a Chronicle play is open to dispute. She might have been greatly surprised by and unable to comprehend some of the dramatist's ideas and interpretations. But she would not have been inclined to cry 'Woe' when this man praised her with his command of stage-craft and of clear, cogent statement. Those who most disagree with Shaw must admit that he was never cloudy or obscure. The play is long but not verbose. Preface and play are models of style, the first in exposition and the second in its vivid, forceful dialogue.

12

D.H. Lawrence : Sons and Lovers

Vividness is what first strikes us in *Sons and Lovers,* the living quality of the novelist's rendering of actuality. Whatever else the novel may attempt, it starts by being solidly rooted in a convincing historical and social setting, and throughout it achieves a quality of vivid authenticity, a live responsiveness to the details of living. One thinks, for example, of Walter Morel at breakfast or cutting fuses with his children, of Mrs. Morel ironing, of Paul collecting his father's money or of Paul and Miriam on the swing.

The scenes thus vividly presented are simultaneously meaningful. In the first two instances we see something of the warmth and vitality of Morel; in the third we see through Paul's eyes both Mrs. Morel's lack of 'fulfilment', which is to place such a strain on her children, and her own vigorous vitality; in the fourth we see Paul's uncertainty and lack of social ease, related to his sense of superiority; the last reveals something of the difference between Paul and Miriam.

Yet a coherent novel offers more than a host of vivid and significant details, and it is to Lawrence's structural organisation of significant detail that I shall now turn. The simple narrative facts, the developing history of the Morel family, provide the novel's basic material, but its meaning cannot emerge till the novel's underlying pattern is grasped.

Much of *Sons and Lovers* derives directly from Lawrence's own experience, but I am not concerned here to note correspondences with or divergences from biographical fact. For whatever its relation to Lawrence's own life, the novel stands on its own feet as imaginative fiction, and it is as such that we should consider it. It is worth noting, however, that Lawrence rewrote the novel several times, that the personal immediacy of the material posed urgent problems to his understanding, and that one of the characteristics of the novel is the sense of experience convincingly presented while still not fully understood.

There is some dispute about the underlying structure and meaning of the novel. The difficulty is, I think, that Lawrence offers two patterns organising the experience of the novel, (with a third perspective which I shall return to later). These two ways of viewing and organising the material of the novel exist simultaneously and this can cause confusion. In the first view, the novel explores Paul's relations with three women, Miriam, Clara and his mother, all of whom have something to offer him, but all of whom have ultimately to be rejected as inadequate. In the second view the novel is the story of a woman unsatisfied in her relation with her husband, who turns to her sons for fulfilment, with the result that they are unable to achieve satisfactory relationships with other women. The first viewpoint emphasises the insufficiency of the women whom Paul loves, the second viewpoint emphasises the insufficiency of Paul himself. Both viewpoints are present in the novel, and I shall examine each in turn.

From Miriam Paul derives stimulus, a deepening of 'insight', and an increase of 'intensity'. Yet from the very start one is made aware of things in Miriam that make a successful relationship between them unlikely. Paul dislikes her overemotional intensity with her youngest brother, her intrusion of 'soul into algebra, her inability to be ordinary and 'jolly'. There is a clenched and timid quality about her. She is frightened of feeding the hens, or riding on the swing, and the scenes anticipate her sexual incapacity. In her self-sacrificial spirituality Paul discerns a persistent possessiveness. As she tries to 'pull the heart out of' the daffodils in the opening of Chapter IX, Paul lashes out at her habit of 'fondling things', of "begging things to love' her. This scene is characteristic of Miriam's anthropomorphic activity, and represents a violation of the integrity of objects in their own right, as her vision of the wild-rose bush is similarly tainted with her subjectivity. At the end of the novel she can only offer Paul sacrificial love, and the relation between them is brought to an end with Miriam 'feeling dead'.

With Clara, Paul experiences the fulfilment of physical passion. This brings him at its best a relation with elemental vitality, with the living force of the whole universe—'They had met, and included in their meeting the thrust of the manifold grass-stems, the cry of the peewit, the wheel of the stars'. Their passion gives them a joy and vitality which radiates to the old lady who gives them tea and who presents Clara with 'three tiny dahlias'. Lawrence vividly captures their infectious glow of delight.

Lawrence's treatment of Paul's relationship with Clara is sketchy outside their sexual relation, but he sketches in two causes of failure in Clara. There is a touch of the personally possessive in her even after the more than personal intensity of passion; she feels 'she had not got him; and there is an inequality between them' (which makes the relation inevitably transitory)—as Paul knows 'it was not she who could keep his soul steady'. The purely sexual relationship lacks sufficient basis, and the relationship inevitably breaks up.

With his mother Paul experiences much of the joy of his youth. They share with real delight her purchase of the corn-flower dish and the pansy roots, and the excitement of their trip to Nottingham. She acts as a stimulus to him in that he does things for her whether blackberrying or painting : 'All his work was hers'. It is her love which saves his life when he nearly dies of pneumonia.

But the cost of her love is high. A full treatment of Mrs. Morel's effect on Paul would consider the quarrel between the Morel parents in detail, for the mother turns the children against the father, and looks to them for fulfilment rather than him. In passing, I would suggest that Lawrence's novel is richer than what seems at times to be his conscious intention. There is a warmth in Morel which frequently shows him to good advantage, for all his failings; and how much this short sentence reveals about his wife—'Mrs. Morel did not like the wakes'.

I shall go on to consider the cost of Mrs. Morel's love to Paul more fully in a moment. Here a sentence may summarise the damage 'her bondage' causes him—'She bore him, loved him, kept him, and his love turned back to her, so that he could not be free to go forward with his own life, really love another woman'. With her death, Paul is at last free of the most subtly undermining of his three loves, all of whom he ultimately rejects.

What I have called the second viewpoint is explained by Lawrence in a letter to Garnett, and shows an obvious correspondence to Freudian psychology. While I think that the novel is too rich and complex to be confined within the limits of a simple formula, the damaging influence of the mother's love is felt throughout the novel, and there are moments in his relations with Miriam and Clara, where an apparent insufficiency in Paul stems from the relation with his mother—'Was *he* deficient in something ? Perhaps he was'. The question comes as he tries to break off with Miriam and a little later we read : 'He had come back to his mother. Here was the strongest tie in his life'. In the relation with Clara, she notices a failure in his loving—'You can't come out of yourself, you can't'. Paul himself sadly observes to his mother of both Miriam and Clara—'You know, I don't care about them, mother'.

Mrs. Morel's dislike of Miriam stems from jealousy and when she upbraids Paul about Miriam the damaging nature of their relation is apparent—'Instinctively he realised that he was life to her. And, after all, she was the chief thing to him, the only supreme thing'. In the anguish of her love for Paul she shows the cause of her misplaced love : 'I've never had a husband—not really', but one is ready to sympathise with Morel's 'vanomously' uttered comment, as he enters—'At your mischief again ?' In a crucial conversation in Chapter XIII, Paul touches 'the quick of the trouble', as he realises he has somehow 'wronged' his women, through being unable to '*give*' himself, and his conclusion is clear—'I shall never meet the right woman while you live'.

Lawrence in his account of the novel suggests that Paul 'is left in the end naked of everything, with the drift towards death'. Certainly this is there, but it is not a full account of the novel's close. From whichever viewpoint we consider the novel, Paul's position at the close is bleak, but there is a vitality in him which may not be ignored. We have been shown this when he is on the swing; talking of his painting; up in the cherry tree; among the flowers of the garden at night; and in the moment of fulfilment with Clara. This vitality may not be discounted, for all the evidence of a contrary movement, a 'lapse towards death'. Again, it should be noted that Paul's administering the overdose of morphia to his mother is both a merciful easing of her torture and also an active breaking of a bond that has become intolerable. Finally, even at the end Paul 'would not admit that he wanted to die'. In the last scene with Miriam it is she rather than he who ends 'feeling dead', while he is associated with his flowers, 'freesias' and 'scarlet anemones'. The last pages offer a vision of darkness, but in the image of the ear of wheat Lawrence offers a hint of renewal, and this is supported by Paul's effect of choice—'he would not give in'.

Whether Paul's experience is seen as the story of three rejected loves, or of the crippling effects of his mother's love, Paul is left frailly alive. It has rightly been noticed that 'quickly', the novel's last word, means not only 'rapidly' but also 'lovingly'.

'This is a constant revelation in Hardy's novels', wrote Lawerence in his *Study of Thomas Hardy*, 'that there exists a great background, vital and vivid, which matters more than the people who move upon it', and it is a constant revelation in Lawrence too. From this comes the third perspective which I mentioned earlier : in this the human actors are seen in relation to the larger life around them. In his rendering of the surrounding world of nature, Lawrence opens a dimension in the novel which we may call religious; yet the scenes which achieve this resonance are achieved with vivid authenticity. I take as illustration the description of Mrs. Morel out in the moonlight among the flowers, dizzied with their scent, and smeared with pollen. The scene is awesome—'The tall white lilies were reeling in the moonlight, and the air was charged with their perfume as with a presence.' Mrs. Morel gasped slightly in fear. One can point to many instances of this kind of scene in *Sons and Lovers*, and they are worth attention. One thinks of the children's games around the solitary lamp-post surrounded by darkness; of the entry of William's coffin through the door 'which opened straight from the night into the room'; of the vision of the wild-rose bush (which is there for all Miriam's tainting subjectivity); and of Paul's vision (as he decides to break with Miriam) of the flowers at night, with the clear note of something achieved—'At any rate, he had found something'. These scenes are central to an understanding of the full perspective of the novel, for they place the human characters in relation to a life that is larger than them, 'a great background, vital and vivid'.

13

E. M. Forster: A Passage To India

A Passage to India was not only the climax of Forster's career as a novelist but can also be seen as one of the high watermarks of the 20th century novel. On the surface it seems an easy novel to read. Unlike Joyce's *Ulysses*, it is not significant for any startling innovations in narrative technique, and indeed many early critics thought of it simply as a late example of the Victorian style of novel-writing. Yet the more we study it, the more we realize that it can be enjoyed on many different levels, and that, far from being a purely traditional type of novel, it is a highly original amalgam of various aspects, the nature of which we shall explore in this essay.

Probably most of us, with any novel, respond first of all to the story. Yet Forster, in one of his lectures, seemed rather to regret the necessity for a story: 'Yes—oh dear yes—the novel tells a story. . . . That is the highest factor common to all novels, and I wish that it was not so, that it could be something different—melody, or perception of the truth. . . .' Nevertheless, *A Passage to India* is a brilliant example of story—telling, which maintains our interest from start to finish in the mere surface actions and yet at the same time allows the writer to say much that is profound about friendship, about the future of a nation, and about religious belief.

The 'Passage' to India is, obviously, that taken by Adela Quested to meet her fiance, Ronny Heaslop (though it means more than this, as we shall see later). Both Adela and her companion, Mrs. Moore, who is Ronny's mother, have a burning desire to see the 'real' India, and from this all the trouble stems. Neither lady shares the prejudices against Indians of most of the British in India, and their behaviour finally stirs up a crisis in the town of Chandrapore.

The pivot on which the action turns is the visit Adela and Mrs. Moore make, at the invitation of a young Muslim doctor, Aziz, to the mysterious Marabar Caves. Mrs. Moore finds the Caves terrifying, for reasons we shall discuss later, and only visits the first. Adela however goes on to visit the rest alone with Aziz and a guide. What happens is never made clear : Adela suddenly rushes in terror down the mountainside, is helped into a car by an acquaintance, Miss Derek, who has just driven up, and is taken back to Chandrapore in a state of extreme shock. The rest of the party carry on with their picnic, but when they arrive back at Chandrapore, Aziz is arrested on a charge of having attacked Adela in one of the Caves.

Some critics have criticised the Caves episode because of the vagueness and mystery which seem to surround it. The puzzle of what happened is never solved. Yet the mysteriousness is appropriate : Forster leaves room for our own imaginations and makes us conscious that there may be more in life than we think. One of his themes, too was that 'India's a muddle', so that the Caves episode is an illustration of this fact. More important still, the Caves episode is essential to the story because it leads on to the trial of Aziz. One of the principal themes of the novel is Anglo-Indian relations and the possibility of two different cultures existing in harmony. It is therefore important for the novel to have some crisis which will bring the problem of Anglo-Indian relations to a head, and this is exactly what the Caves episode and the whole subsequent action which culminates in the trial do. We see how both the British and the Indians react under intense emotional stress, and neither side comes out well. The British appear at their most begoted, imperialistic and hysterical, while the Indians, especially after the trial, are seen to be cynical and hard. To some extent they have a right to be, since they have a just grievance, but even so our opinion of Aziz and his friends cannot help being lowered.

The other important point about the story concerns Part III. By the end of Part II, Mrs. Moore is dead, Adela has decided not to marry Ronny and to return to England, Fielding, the College Principal and friend of Aziz has also returned to England, and Aziz has left Chandrapore to take charge of a hospital in one of the Native States. To all intents and purposes the story seems to be finished, but because Forster wanted to do much more than just tell a story, he needed Part III to round off the work. This is where, finally, Fielding, with Mrs. Moore's other two children, Stella and Ralph, meets Aziz again, and where, against a background of ritual celebrations of Krishna's birth and in the life-renewing rains of the monsoon, a reconciliation is attempted. In the end, however, it does not seem to work. 'No, not yet', the earth seems to say, and the sky says 'No, not there'. These are the novel's closing words, as if to say that neither the place nor the time are right for Englishman and Indian to become friends.

A Passage to India can also be enjoyed as a story set against a national and historical background of considerable importance. Forster began to write it at the time of his first visit to India, but did not complete it until after the First World War, so that the atmosphere of the book reflects the days of Edwardian imperialism, at the same time as it looks forward to the years leading up to Independence in 1947. Forster's attitude is not a narrow one, and as we read we instinctively feel that what he writes is universally true and, in a sense, prophetic. All of his previous novels except for *The Longest Journey* had dealt with the clash of two cultures. In *A Room with a View* and *Where Angels Fear to Tread* it was

England and Italy; in *Howard's End* it was England and Germany. In *A Passage to India* the theme is quite clearly stated in Chapter 2, where Aziz and his friends are discussing 'whether or no *it is possible to be friends with an Englishman*'. This leads us also to Forster's preoccupation with the importance of personal relations, for *A Passage to India* is not merely about a conflict between the indigenous culture and that imposed by the ruling nation ('The roads, named after victorious generals and intersecting at right angles, were symbolic of the net Great Britain had thrown over India'.), but is also a novel about a search for friendship. This is seen both in the fast-ripening confidence between Aziz and Mrs. Moore, born of his first meeting with her in the Mosque and lasting beyond her death, and in the relationship of Aziz and Fielding. The story supports this theme over and over by showing how chance events can make or mar friendships, and by underlining their fragility. How much rests on a borrowed collar-stud; how much is shattered when Aziz misreads Fielding's letter and thinks he is married to Adela. In Mrs. Moore's case that chance encounter in the Mosque had given a promise of renewal, awakened her to a 'sudden sense of unity, of kinship with the heavenly bodies', which passed into the old woman and out, like 'water through a tank, leaving a strange freshness behind'. Yet all this is lost as a result of her nightmare experience in the Caves. Afterwards she is remote from everyone, a sick and peevish old woman who dies alone on the boat taking her back to England.

The negative aspect of the clash between cultures is seen in the attitude of the Anglo-Indians, the Turtons and McBrydes and Callendars, to the Indians they govern. While the Englishmen respect their subordinates—otherwise they would have to accept that their careers had been 'a bad investment'—the women are a restraining influence, clinging to their traditions, intensifying the colour-bar, and dreading any encroachment on their power by the Indians. Adela realizes this when she fears that she 'would sea India always as a frieze never as a spirit'.

This negative aspect is shown most fully at the 'Bridge Party' arranged by the Turtons so that Adela and Mrs. Moore may meet their 'Aryan brother'. The result is merely for the shy Indian ladies and their menfolk to gather at one end of the lawn and the English at the other. Finally the English commander all the tennis courts, and although Mrs. Turton attempts to be civil to her Indian guests she is hardly successful: 'She had learnt the lingo, but only to speak to her servants, so she knew none of the politer forms and of the verbs only the imperative mood'. Even when Adela tries to cross this 'bridge' she fails, for she finds herself striving in vain against the 'echoing walls of their civility'—a curious foreshadowing of her experience in the Caves.

Forster once spoke of *A Passage to India* as a 'passage for Indians' as well as English. In other words, it could be seen as a search for identity as a nation. On the one hand we have the Muslim Aziz, deeply conscious of India's past glories under the Mogul emperors and sensitive to the poetry of Islam—and on the other the Brahman Godbole, and between them they represent the two opposing tendencies : of a narrow nationalism and of a philosophical comprehension of man and his place in nature which seems to embrace all mankind. Chapters 30 and 31 are of interest in this connection, since they show some of the reactions to the idea of a unified India and some of the insuperable difficulties. Aziz sums up the whole problem, too, at the very end when he says to Fielding "We may hate one another, but we hate you most. . . we shall get rid of you, yes, we shall drive every blasted Englishman into the sea, and then. . . you and I shall be friends'.

The question of the national and historical background leads us to a third aspect of Forster's novel, for while the theme of Anglo-Indian relations is an extremely serious one, this does not prevent *A Passage to India* from being, on a grand scale, a social comedy—Just as Forster's earliest novels had been. The novel of social comedy is indeed a peculiarly English genre, familiar from Jane Austen to Charles Dickens. Even George Eliot, in *The Mill on the Floss*, had combined a serious theme with deliciously comic observation of character. Forster's work is thus no innovation. His comic sense is most obvious in the way he caricatures the Anglo-Indians, often with biting satirs, as when he says of Ronny that he 'approved of religion as long as it endorsed the National Anthem'. The English are not the whole flat characters at whom he deliberately pokes fun, whereas the Indians are portrayed in more detail—especially Aziz—and with affectionate understanding.

Forster's comic vision extends not only to portraits of people and their ways but to whole episodes in the novel, for instance the trial scene where the English all crowd on to the dais with their chairs, hiding the magistrate from view, and have to be sent off again. The best episodes of all in this respect are the train journey to the Marabar Hills and the Festival of Gokul Ashtami in Part III, for as Forster wisely says, '*there is fun in heaven*'. *By sacrificing good taste* Hinduism had achieved what Christianity had shirked, 'the inclusion of merriment' Forster was never charitable in his writings towards bigoted, narrow, hard-hearted people, but if we look at his work as a whole we can see that his comic vision is more than mere poking fun. His comprehension of human nature is greater than this, so that he passes no judgment, and in the end the reader feels sympathy for Ronny Heaslop and even for McBryde, in their human weakness.

Forster's comic vision is inevitably expressed in his style. His characteristic 'tone of voice' often seems to be one of levity, deliberately unemphatic and off-hand: 'the Ganges happens not to be holy here'. He describes Godbole in a turban that looked like 'pale purple macaroni' or tells us that 'the train slowed up against an elephant'. Some critics have regretted his tendency to buttonhole the reader in a rather Victorian way : 'Visions are supposed to entail profundity, but—Wait till you get one, dear reader !' Some are puzzled too by the odd mingling of comedy and high seriousness in both the style and the themes of the novel. Undoubtedly this double attitude exists, and we may interpret it as a typically British capacity for masking deep feeling by under-statement and irony. Yet the virtue of his style is in its vividness and lightness. Detail is piled upon detail so that we see and hear and smell India and are absolutely convinced, but never bored.

And when Forster portrays a scene like that in the garden room at the Government College, or the courthouse, or the lakeside ceremony at Mau, there is a warmth and colour and completeness in his descriptions which could scarcely be surpassed.

At this point we may well feel that there is ample justification for according *A Passage to India* considerable importance as a novel. But to appreciate it to the full we need also to consider both its construction and its religious themes, and to see why it is regarded as an outstanding symbolical novel.

Forster arranged his novel in three parts corresponding both to aspects of religion and to the Indian year : part I, Mosque, takes place in the cool season; part II, Caves, in the hot, dry season; part III, Temple, brings us to the life-renewing rains. Within this framework, which not only contrasts Hinduism and Islam but also shows the predicament of the Christian (through Mrs. Moore and her vision in the Cave), Forster builds up a very complex network of allusions. We have already noticed the reference to 'echoing walls', an idea made fact when the party visits the Caves. The Marabar Hills, too, recur like a theme in music, ominous and strange. Then there is the odd incident when the Nawab Bahadur's car collides with some mysterious creature in the darkness and its alarmed occupants are rescued by Miss Derek in her car. This is paralleled in Adela's experience in the Caves—we never know what bumped into her—and in her rescue by Miss Derek. Then again, there is the wasp Mrs. Moore sees on the coatpeg, which reappears in Godbole's thoughts in Part III—'One old Englishwoman and one little, little wasp. . . It does not seem much, still it is more than I am myself'. The result is not only to unify this long novel but also to lend to things and events a significance greater than is at first apparent, and this brings us to the whole idea of symbolism in the novel.

Put simply, a symbol in a novel may be a person, thing, place, happening—anything which has a significance greater than, or different from its obvious meaning, and can therefore convey some truth the writer wishes to express. And in writing his novel he will tend to make the whole story and the portrayal of his characters serve this end. This is true of *A Passage to India*, for the title means not only an actual passage on a ship, and a 'passage' to nationhood, but also a passage for the soul, and this is symbolized in the visit to the Caves, and in the nightmare experience of the echo which Mrs. Moore has in them. Obviously there is nothing special about the Caves, for although Godbole seems nonplussed when asked to describe them, Forster states in Chapter 12 that they are readily described. In fact they are all alike and quite insignificant, but they have one claim to beauty—a miraculous effect of light on the polished stone when a match is struck. Mrs. Moore sees none of this, however, but only hears the echo, an echo which seems to undermine her hold on life, to speak to her of all that is mean and small in nature and human relations, to rob the universe of its vastness. It evokes too her reflections on the goodness and love of God and, perhaps, because she is old, and unwell, and physically overcome by the sun and stench, the barrenness of the hills and the darkness of the Cave, doubt and unbelief assail her. Afterwards her life seems to have lost all joy and peace, and she descends into a kind of hell, 'the twilight of the double vision in which so many elderly people are involved'.

If the effect of the echo were to end there we should have little reason for calling it a symbol, but in fact it acquires a life of its own in the novel. Adela goes on to explore the Caves in a matter-of-fact way, and is not immediately conscious of any horror—but afterwards she is. For the whole period leading up to the trial the echo haunts her, right until she admits that Aziz was innocent. Even Fielding is not immune from it: 'Everthing echoes now; there no stopping the echo. The original sound may be harmless, but the echo is always evil'. This reflection... lay at the verge of Fielding's mind. 'He could never develop it. It belonged to the universe that he had missed or rejected'. It is as though Mrs. Moore has had an almost psychic influence on the action; the echo passes from her to others, but her influence is ultimately for good. She has indeed been called a 'guardian', in this sense, for it is through almost telepathically received hints from her—

words Adela thinks, but is not sure, she hears her utter—that Adela comes to retract her accusation. As a guardian, too, she is linked with Godbole, who seems to symbolize the absolute comprehension and assimilation of the universe. Where Mrs. Moore's experience is one of black anguish, Godbole's represents the achievement of total spiritual harmony.

What conclusions Forster draws about religion and the meaning of existence it is not easy to determine. Fielding, the acknowledged 'black atheist', is conscious of a universe 'missed or rejected', and he seems nearest as inadequate for him—"There is no God but God" doesn't carry us far through the complexities of matter and spirit. . . a religious pun, not a religious truth'—just as for Aziz the ceremony of Gokul Ashtami is meaningless, an 'annual antic'. The Hindu religion is all-embracing—even of the Christian 'God si ove', misspelled—but for this very reason it lacks order and only reflects the muddle of India. Truth in the end seems unattainable, and even the matter-of-fact Fielding and Adela, as they say goodbye, feel wistfulness descending on them—'the shadow of the shadow of a dream fell over their clear-cut interests, and objects never seen again seemed messages from another world'.

A Passage to India has been seen as a novel of reconciliation, but while it has a grand unity of design, and a wise comprehensiveness, it is hard to accept that its final word is one of optimism. The message of the echo is one of a despair that is never exercised. Aziz and Fielding never again become friends; no one religion provides a satisfactory antidote to the nightmare of meaninglessness; and if there is any hope at all it is only in the character of Ralph and Stella, whom we insufficiently see. Forster leaves us with a question mark over the future, in a vast and unsatisfactory landscape with its hundred voices, and under that over-arching sky :

> 'Some Kites hovered overhead, impartial; over the Kites passed the mass of a vulture, and with an impartiality exceeding all, the sky, not deeply coloured but trans-

> lucent, poured light from its whole circumference. It seemed unlikely that the series stopped here. Beyond the sky must not there be something that overarches all the skies, more impartial even than they? Beyond which again. . .'

and if he gives any answer at all it can only be 'a compromise between destiny and desire'.

14

Vision and Form in Literature

Since my intention in this paper is to attempt a definition of literature, I should perhaps state at the very outset that I regard with suspicion any definition of art which claims to be either normative or comprehensive. The essence of literature as I conceive it depends upon the existence of a kind of literature to which I have been receptive. Since there is much literature I am ignorant of and since there is also a large body of literature to which I have been unable to attune myself, my concept of literature is necessarily a limited concept. And so too, I believe, is the concept of anyone else.

Literature, as we all know, has many definitions. And were I asked why literature has so many definitions, I should suggest, it is because it preserves a perennial vitality and resists being defined once and for all. If here I am trying to give one more definition of literature it is not because I am so presumptuous as to suppose that I have found the final answer to the elusive question, what is literature; but because, I feel that the dialectics out of which my definition has emerged as a synthesis—or rather, into which it gets ramified-might help in the understanding of the nature of a kind of literature which qualitatively is not too insignificant. To come to my definition then, literature is intuition transmitted as intuition through the medium of words.

I shall try to explain the nature of intuitive perception with the help of a simple illustration from Frost:

> The old dog barks backward without getting up.
> I can remember when he was a pup.

Frost calls this "The Span of Life". In the poem, the first line focusses the reader's attention on the dog at a particular moment in time. The second line sees the dog at another, much earlier moment, but a moment which is ironically related to the first. In the life of the dog the two moments do not exist together but, in the perception of Frost, they do, along with the ironical relationship which binds them and which, though not made explicit, is implied in the juxtaposition.

The intuitive capacity is this capacity to simultaneously perceive things than stand apart in time and space and are yet bound together by certain relationships. Intuition grasps complexities *on mass* by perceiving a unity in them. It is a synthetic process that sees things together, as if they existed in space. It is unlike logic which breaks down complexities into simpler units and tries to understand them bit by bit through analysis and which sees things in a sequence as though they existed in time. The artist's method of perception is intuitive in nature. He aims at a simultaneous perception of many related things. Modern critical terms like ambiguity, paradox and tension show that contemporary critics are intensely aware of the unification of multiplicities which an art-work achieves. If we look at a lyric like Tennyson's "Break, Break, Break", which is somewhat longer than Frost's poem, there too we see the same process at work. The dashing of the breakers against the shore, the cold grey stones, the fisherman's boy playing with his sister, the sailor lad singing in his boat, the stately ships moving over the waters, the memory of vanished hands and the grief caused by Hallam's internal tensions of contrasts and harmony.

Even when we move on to larger literary forms—the epic or the novel—the nature of the art-work does not change.

Experiences in time and experiences in space are formed into a structure, which *is* the novel, and that structure stands *en bloc* carved out of absolute time. By absolute time I mean time in the chunk, as a congealed mass, and not time on the move. It is time that has acquired a property of space—extension. The real experience of a novel starts not when we are regarding it but when the reading is over. While reading the novel, we might get interested in the textural beauties, that is in the beauty of the parts, and we may also feel impelled to go on reading the novel till the end by a curiosity to know what happens. But the curiosity to know what happens is ephemeral and ends with the reading and the textural beauties become subsidiary to the structure. A reader sees a novel in its entirety only after he has read it through. Then as he turns the pages and reads snatches at random, his memories of the different parts keep merging and relations between part and part keep unfolding themselves to him and he moves towards a fuller understanding of the novel. This probably is the reason why a sensitive reader cannot take up a new novel immediately after finishing one. First he has to live through an intense experience, the perception of a complex totality.

Coleridge defined "the Beautiful" as "that in which the many, still seen as many, becomes one". This definition shows that the Beautiful in art is a product of the intuitive perception, for the synthesis demanded by it cannot be achieved by reason.

A poem by Mr. Archibald MacLeish too bears out my suggested definition of literature. In it he writes:

> A poem should be motionless in time
> As the moon climbs
> Leaving, as the moon releases
> Twig by twig the night-entangled trees,
> Leaving, as the moon behind the winter leaves,
> Memory by memory the mind—
> A poem should be motionless in time
> As the moon climbs[1]

A poem is "motionless in time" because its existence is in absolute time. And just as the twigs and the leaves released by the moon do not fade out but stand as a pattern silhouetted against the moon, only revealed in sequence, but existing simultaneously, even so the memories released by a poem do not dissolve as they come up but stand as a structure held together by the poem, in the poem.

The inspiration theory of creativity held by the old Greeks, and by Longinus, Shakespeare (in *A Midsummer Night's Dream*), Blake, Shelley and others also testifies to the truth of my definition. The supernatural has to be invoked to explain creativity because creativity, being intuitive, lies far beyond rational understanding.

I have said that a novelist presents his vision of life through the *structure* of his novel. Some perhaps hold that he does it through character. Let us see how things happen in *The Brothers Karamazov*. In the book, Ivan posseses the intellectual nihilist's point of view. These are the problems of an 'outsider'. In the book too, besides many others, there is Father Zossima, and Aloysha, both believers in Christian love and in life affirmation. Who embodies Destoyevski's vision? To say Aloysha would be too superficial an answer. I agree that had there been no Aloysha and no Father Zossima, *The Brothers Karamazov* would have been as great a novel as Camus *Outsider*, but not greater. But had there been no Ivan in it, the novel would have degenerated into sentimentality. It is the *juxtaposition* of the two points of view (actually of many more points of view), held together in the novel by their very polarity, that constitutes the vision of Dostoyevski. His vision includes the two extremes of intellectual nihilism and absolute faith, of life negation and life-affirmation.[2] His vision is a kind of *Vishvarupadarshan*. But let me not digress. Coming to the point, juxtaposition is structure, not character. The same is true of a play like *King Lear*, where every character, every incident in the plot, every image of its poetry, is an integral part of the dramatists' vision. In *War and Peace* too none of the major characters, taken individually, incarnates Tolstoi's vision. That vision is constituted of all of them, and much more besides, taken together. Even the soldier who appears just once in the novel only to be tied to a tree and shot before his fellow prisoner Pieere and who just before he is short shifts his feet to a more comfortable position, is a part of Tolstoi's total vision. His role in *War and Peace* is as important for the human totality as that of King Lear's line in *King Lear*: "Pray you, undo this button."[3]

In this book, Tolstoi weaves into a much wider mass movement, the lives and personal problems of individuals. The lives of individuals seen in a much wider context give us a glimpse into the insignificance of human effort. And the forces of wider mass movements converging on individuals made us feel history more immediately. It is structure then, each part seen in the context of the whole, that embodies a writer's vision.

Though I have been talking a lot about structure or form, I believe, the great writer is not primarily concerned with it. The writer who believes in formalism is doomed to mediocrity for form should come naturally and inevitably with the intuition; for, as Croce says, the spirit intuits only in expressing. Wherever intuition operates to converge "the many, still seen as many" into "one", form is bound to arise there.

The major tension in literature is between the vision, and the form that both incarnates and resists it. In the minor writers one feels conscious of the form arching like a ceiling over the vision and containing it. The great writer transcends form. His vision rises like a flame with the form as far as the form will go. Beyond that it sends the heat up through suggestions and vibrations. Formally, *War and Peace* does not concern itself with experiences outside Russia during and for a while after the Napoleonic wars. And yet the reverberations within that space-time form are such that the novel seems to involve all humanity. We do not feel the same way about Jane Austen. In her works we are very conscious of the left outs. And Tolstoi's achievement is due not merely to the size of his novel. Sophocles and Shakespeare achieved the same effect though their works are much smaller in size. Browning's Andrea del Sarto looks at Raphael's painting and says, "That arm is wrongly put". He finds "a fault to pardon in the drawing's lines". And yet looking at the painting he adds:

> But all the play, the insight and the stretch—
> Out of me! out of me![4]
> × × × ×
> There hurns a truer light of God in them,
> ....
> ....than goes on to prompt
> This low-pulsed forthright craftsman's band of mine.[5]

There are times, when as gestalt psychology says, the whole is greater than the sum of its parts. The vision of an artist is the whole; the form is the sum of the parts. The ode is the vision; the strophe, the antistrophe and the epode constitute the form. The novel is the vision; the sum of the chapters, the form.

I have said that literature is intuition transmitted as intuition through the medium of words. The philosopher too often apprehands things by intuition. But he differs from the artist in that he transmits his understanding after translating his institution into logic. Perhaps the *Vedas,* the Bible and Nietgsche are exceptions, but in being exceptions they have become great not only as philoshpy but also as literature.

Though a part of the answer has already been given indirectly, the question, how is one to know that a vision has been transmitted as intuition, merits a more detailed answer. First of all, I know it as I read through a work of art, by the new meanings that the earlier parts acquire as I see them in the light of the later parts. In a logical development of an idea, the earlier parts form the foundation for the later parts. But in an intuitional presentation there is both forward and backward illumination. It is only after one reads the complete poem, the complete story, or the complete play that the various parts fall into place. Such is not the case with the theorem of Pythagoras which builds up in a straight line.

Besides, in a purely logical development only the intellect operates. Such a development may be described as movement in a single strand. But intuition, being a much deeper experience, involves the total personality—the intellectual, the emotional and even the physical. When intuition, therefore, is transmitted as intuition, the transmission has a more complex and a richer texture.

With the coming into vogue of Metaphysical poetry there has been much talk regarding the fusion of the intellect and emotion in literature. What I am concerned with here is how even the physical personality enters literature alongwith the intellectual and the emotional. It does so as rhythm. Rhythm in literature is the physical response to a state of emotion or contemplation investing the feeling and the vision with the attributes of life—motion and energy. Rhythm is the language of dance, the most physical of the arts, where the body, flung into rhythms, finds expression. In the intuitive process too rhythm is deeply involved. The respiration of the sage in meditation is more rhythmic than ordinary respiration. The dancer dancing before the deity realises the ecstasy of worship through the rhythm of her dance.[6] And great poetry too, indeed all creative utterance, first enthralls the body with its rhythm. In his lecture on *The Name and Nature of Poetry*, it was perhaps this that made Housman say that poetry is "more physical than intellectual" and that he felt poetry in "the pit of the stomach". Perhaps the same reason made Coleridge think that poetry is best appreciated when not very well understood. The letters of Tagore, now published, tell us that usually the tunes of his songs came to him before the words,[7] as often to Swinburne. And Flaubert too has left us written evidence that he kept changing the words of his sentences till he got the rhythm right.[8] When Blackmur talks of the use of language as gesture in great poetry, I feel, what he means is the coupling or rhythm with meaning or the making of rhythm itself so pregnant with meaning that word meaning becomes inconsequential. He chooses Macbeth's "Tomorrow and tomorrow" as an example of where words "get out of mere verbal meaning" and "become gesture". He suggests that had

Macbeth said "Today and today and today" instead, "much the same effect (would) have transpired."[9] I think, both the repetitive words are able to create the same effect because, through repetition, both are able to convey the rhythm of ennui and of the feeling to being dragged through life. Even the solitude contemplation becomes meaningful when, as in 'Tintern Abbey', a great rhythm beats through it. A silence that is rhythmless is the silence of the dead. Poetry is "The *Rhythmical Creation of Beauty*"[10] said Poe (the italics are Poe's) and Mr. Archibald MacLeish wrote :

> A poem should be wordless
>
> As the flight of birds[11]

That word *flight* is significant. Symbolishing wordless motion, rhythm at once activises and makes redundant the meaning of words in poetry, by breaking down their fixities and their rigid semantic contours, giving them the fluidity of evocation. Through this fluidity the poet's intuition can move freely through space and time, synthesising all experience. Also, through the motion or rhythm, the dialectics of literary creation is fully realised, for rhythm projects in sequence the the simultaneity of the intuitive perception; it helps us to hear in time the heart-beat of the timeless.

At the conclusion of my paper I wish to thank most of all Mr. Y. Sahai from whom I have received most of my ideas concerning literature and under whose influence my attitude to literature has found shape. Mr. Sahai very kindly looked into the manuscript of my paper and made valuable suggestions. The previous paragraph which comments on Mr. MacLeish's lines and defines the nature of rhythm is almost a transcription of Mr. Sahai's ideas. To him I can never be sufficiently grateful. I am also extremely grateful to Mr. R.N. Deb whom I told the argument of my paper and who then suggested to me an interpretation of *The Brothers Karamazov* (vide Reference 2) that would never have struck me. Moving on from my teachers to a student, I should like to thank Miss Mrinal Pant whose sensitive remark—'Wherever

I perceive rhythm I feel like translating it into dance'—made me vividly realise that rhythm is a physical response. Her remark, quoted here, may serve as an evidence in support of one of my contentions.

REFERENCES

1. Archibald MacLeish, 'Ars Poetics', *Collected Poems 1917-1952* (Houghton Mifflin Co.). The poem is included in *A Pocket Book of Modern Verse*, edited by Oscar Williams (rev. ed.) (New York: Washington Square Press, Inc., Feb., 1964), pp. 373-74.
2. Mr. R.N. Deb offered me an interesting interpretation of *The Brothers Karamazov*:
   Aloysha, Ivan and Dimitri symbolise the spiritual, the intellectual, and the sensuous man. Aloysha is closer to Dimitri than to Ivan because the human spirit has greater affinities with human instincts and senses than with the intellect.
3. *King Lear*, V, III, 311.
4. Robert Browning, 'Andrea del Sarto', *The Poems and Plays of Robert Browning* (New York : The Modern Library, Inc), pp. 218-23, lines 116-17.
5. *Ibid.*, lines 79-82.
6. In the last paragraph of his lecture on *The Religion of an Artist*, Tagore defined dance as "ecstatic meditation in the still centre of movement". That stillness at the centre of movement is possible only because the movement of dance is rhythmic. Rhythm points to a central harmony which is unruffled and where the mind of the dancer can get lost in ecstatic meditation.
7. *Vide*, Rabindranath Tagore, letter to Indiradevi dated 10th Sept., 1894, *Chinnapatravali* (Calcutta : Visvabharati Granthalaya, 1960), pp. 331-32. Also vide, Prabhat Kumar Mukhopadhyaya, *Rabindra-jivani* (4 vols.; Calcutta: Visvabharati Granthalaya, 1359 (1952-53 A.D.), Vol. III, p. 292.
8. "Flaubert without his music is simply not Flaubert. He thought so much of the music of what he wrote that he conceived his *chutes des pharases*, his 'dying falls' as we may call them, before he found the words to attach to them. In other words, and quite plainly and simply, he conceived the sound first and the words afterwards."—

translator's 'Introduction', Gustave Flaubert, *Madame Bovary*, translated by J. Lewis May (London and Glasgow : Collins, 1953), p. 16.

9. R.P. Blackmur, *Language as Gesture* (London : Allen and Unwin, 1961), p. 13.

10. Edgar Allan Poe, 'The Poetic Principle, '*American Critical Essay*'s *XIX-XX Century*, edited by Norman Foerster (London : Oxford University Press, 1930), p. 10.

11. MacLeish, 'Ars Poetics'.

15

The Realistic Novel and the Lost Dimension

The novel has become the most dominant form in modern literature and, like other forms, has taken a course of its own—singular and striking. As modern poetry broke away largely from tradition for new semantic and emotional values, and the modern drama from the naturalistic to the poetic play and then to the play of ideas, so the novel has passed from tried forms to a new one in which crime, sex, violence, and breaking of all moral and social codes predominate. Our age is obsessed with the unnatural and with protest against society and morality. There was a time when people were interested in the social milieu and the surface of life and in a story well-told. Then came a revolution in which novelists were interested in inward life and cycles being. This last was the kind of novel which appealed to Bloomshbury and the highbrows of literacy circles preoccupied with findings in psychoanalysis. The latest and sharpest change in public taste is for the novel of shock the novel of protest—the Blood and Guts school of writing.

To people of intense awareness and even to dull and bored ones, these novels indicate, in the best way possible, the consciousness of our age and the predicament of our civilization and our century. Two World Wars have played havoc with the unconscious minds of the younger generations of the decades immediately following them. In World War I the young intellectuals marched out from the fields of Oxford and Cambridge and Yale and Harvard to the Western Front with a song on their lips—burning with patriotism and an idealism to "Keep the World Safe for Democracy". At the end of the War those who returned had left behind in the mud of Flanders, their ideals and accepted values. Amidst this debacle of moral confusion and disillusion the younger generation came into its own. It brought with it an uncompromising revolt against all moral tradition; an undeceiving veneer of pseudosophistication; and a pathetic cry of barren and bleak frustration. This was the lost generation described so vividly by Hemingway in that despairing book "The Sun also Rises".

Noisy, blatant and callous, the utterances of the lost generation fooled none but the members of the young generation themselves; but the movement must still be reckoned with as affording general perspective on the general spirit of futile protest which pervades most of our literature even to-day.

It might be well to adduce a few specific examples from the novels of the twenties and thirties. In Scott Fitzerald's '*This Side of Paradise*', Amory Blair cries out : "Life is a *damned muddle . . . a football game with everyone offside* and the referee gotten rid off". "Life is so much spilt milk", says Margret Wade in Robert Nathan's 'Autumn'. A character in Glenway Westcott's '*The Apple of the Eye*' says that—"the purpose of life is to go on, just to go on". Without significant expression all the characters in Theodore Dreiser's books are merely puppets in a harsh world; and Dreiser himself contineuely refers to "the undertow of this clanking farce called life". How easy it would be to extend the list of quotations! But from what I have already said it becomes clear that this literature of self-depreciation has manifested itself chiefly in two ways : in an over-developed social consciousness which has made a good deal of literature mere propaganda and not art; and in that break of tradition and form zealously followed by members of the younger generations in revolt against everything—including revolt itself.

A further aspect of this literature of negation was the beginning of a preoccupation with sex. D.H. Lawrence may perhaps be considered the high priest of this school of writing. He was a philosophy of protest against accepted social institutions and mores. "The whole scheme of things", he says in a letter to Charles Wilson, "is unjust and rotten, and money is just a disease upon humanity. It's time there was an *enormous* revolution not to instal Soviets but to give life itself a chance". The primary concern of Lawrence was to safeguard the integrity of individual personality against the various manifestations of collectivism in recent times and he is inexhorably led on to a glorification of sex. According to Lawrence, it is during the uninhibited play of this elemental passion between men and women that they attain the fullness of their lives. "Uninhibited" is the word best used to describe the sexual scenes in 'Lady Chatterley's Lover'. Since Lady Chatterley, intimate sexual disclosures in the novel have become common place. Many would say that the novel has thus gained in truth and honesty. Perhaps taboos and restrictions are a block to the serious writer, but the removal of them does not guarantee an improvement in the quality of the novel.

Across the Atlantic in America this obsession with social protest and sex of the lost generation found expression in a new technique in the novels of John Dos Passos whose first novel was described by one critic as an explosion in a cesspool. Dos Passos's technique has been described as 'Panoramic' and 'Kaleidoscopic'—words which we associate with the modern wide cinema screen. Yet his characters sound the deepest notes of futility and disillusionment against a sordid background of promiscuous sex, bad booze and violent deaths. Particularly significant of the confusion in the world of Dos Passos is the fact that most of the central characters are sexually frigid, deprived or frustrated. Where the sexual life is presumed to be satisfactory Dos Passos ignores it. His idealism, if he has any, has, therefore, lost its hold on fact. The result shows the facts in the stream of materialism as grim dark and uncontrollable, whereas the optimism of the spirit is wasted in fierce yet futile indignation.

And while the angry young men of the thirties screamed and brandished their fists in protest the world drifted into the greatest conflagration ever—World War II.

The Second World War presented a mirror to the human condition which blinded anyone who looked into it. For if tens of millions were killed in concentration camps out of the inexorable agonies and contractions of injustice of totalitarian states, one was then obliged also to see that no matter how crippled and perverted an image of man was the society he had created it was nonetheless his creation, and if society was so murderous who could then ignore asking the same hideous question about this own nature.

And the questions were asked by reactionaries of the post-war period who survived the nightmares of the war to awaken to a post-war world that had no place for them. In America was born the new Bonemian—the hipster and the beatnik—the one who refuses to conform—the philosophical psychopath. They questioned and they dared not to conform. They wanted to touch at the blood-roots of man's self and experience, and celebrated the physical and the sexual. Their effort is to produce an expression that is absolutely disinfected from Art and Ideas, an expression that is freed from all tradition and from anything remembered as literature. Then only Art acceptable to these New Romantic savages is the Art of unconsciousness of Accident, of no meaning. And hence they constantly write about those parts of experience which are beneath the level of the critical mind or the culture-consciousness: sexuality, narcotic vision, or the bare sequences in a stream of images. It is not possible here to examine all the writers of this school. I shall, therefore, restrict myself briefly to two.

The one-time leader, philosopher, and pace-setter of the best Generation is Norman Mailer whose two best known works are '*The Naked and the Dead*' written shortly after the war and *The Deer Park* written in the mid-fifties. "Please do not understand me too quickly" warns Mailer. There is not much to understand in either of these works where the prose and the sex and the violence flow thick. This seemed forgivable in *The Naked and the Dead* : a jungle platoon in world war II

("Kinsay's Army" as one reviewer called it) was not supposed to talk like lady members of a book club. But in *The Deer Park* set in Hollywood the ladies talk just like the boys in the jungle as well as act like the animals in it. And at the end of twelve hundred pages which the two books roughly cover one is left with a sense that the lives in it have been wasted and Mailer cannot find a way preventing this waste. After an absence of several years during which his personal life took on the frenzy of the characters of his novels, Mailer published in 1965 '*An American Dream*'. The hero murders his wife, seduces her maid to give himself an alibi and for the rest of the book takes the reader on a nightmare journey through every imaginable evil.

Nelson Algren writes warmly and sympathetically of the ruined lives of drunks and drug-addicts and hobos in the city jungles. Algren's aim is to show that his characters stripped to the core of survival have no strength, or use for 'complicated emotions'—prestige and vanity. According to Algren they have the 'clear simple emotion': hunger, fear, sex and despair—near the bone of life where the individual can know what he feels is true. Algre seems to have given up completely any hope that society can be improved or purified. The only innocents are his bums and derelicts in the jungle of viciousness. '*The Man with the Golden Arm*' his best known work may move and move deeply many a reader, but it must be finally regarded as irresponsible and inaccurate—a sentimental contravence that has little to do with reality and merely explores a blind alley in the writers's imagination.

Miller, Mailer, Kerouse, Burroughs, Styron, Algren and others of the Solar Plexus and groin school of writers are voices crying a sterile philosophy in the asphalt jungles of out teeming cities. They do not conform—they are critical—they protest—but what do they have to offer instead, these rebel without a cause? What they have to offer could perhaps be best illustrated by a quotation from Harold Robbins', '*Never Love a Stranger*' where towards the end of the book the hero remarks : "But what about me? I had never turned to look inside myself. What about me? Of all the people I knew myself least of all. Why did I do things? What did I want? Why did I drift, never really searching for an answer to myself? I wondered. What did I want? Money? Love? Friends? Respect? I searched through my mind for the answer, but none was forthcoming.

Ours is a sorry age, full of, in the words of Alex Comfort 'a world-wide twentieth century fear'. We have vast and proliferating cities in an atomic age, with every modern convenience and amenity, but what is lacking is serenity of spirit and integrity of life. The individual is submerged in political systems highly mechanized and tending to statolatry to the disregard of the fundamental human rights. All this leads, in extreme cases to the making of individuals into murders and criminals, neurotics and perverts. These wrecks of humanity fill our penitentiaries and their corpses lie often in our morgue for police reports and coroner's findings : they also move about in the everyday world, and although they do not murder and do not commit offence normalogically, are involved in schemes of mental torture and sadistic activities against people who live with them and under them. Psychology has influenced novelists to present certain neurotic patterns as almost universal. Psychiatry, it has been aptly said, makes all characters one. Violence has become a sensational end in itself.

Slim tied Riley to a tree. Slim grinned. He liked to see people squirm and turn yellow with fear. He pulled Riley's shirt and bared his belly. Riley gasped and begged—No Slim No. For God's sake don't . . . . Don't do it ! But Slim only grinned and the knife went in slowly as if it were going into butter. Slim watched and revelled in the slow death and aquinted at his victim and said "Take your time, Pal". It is this killer who is involved in a sexual horror story with the kidnapped daughter of a millionaire in James Hadley Chase's '*No Orchards for Miss Blandish*'. And yet this book received rave reveiws and was the first in a long line of successful glory crime thrillers, from Raymond Chandler and Daniel Hammett to Mickey Spilllance and Ian Fleming, appealing to the jaded tastes of the sensational hungry public.

This then is the trend of our century. How does the Catholic writer fit into this scheme of things? Here we touch upon a problem which has exercised, and still exercises, not only the critic but the novelist—the problem of the flesh and sin in the Catholic novel. Certainly the animal side of man, its activities and effects on human life, constitute an element of reality. Man's sextual life is a fact that must be reckoned with, as all but universal fact. Sin and evil is the reality around us. How can the Catholic novelist be of this age and yet something more?

To find the answer I would like to turn to a more detailed examination of the works of Graham Greene. Greene believed that religion was a precious factor in the modern novel. He traced that in his essay on Francois Mauriac (another great Catholic novelist in the Greene tradition) where he refers to Henry James : "With the death of James the religious sense was lost in the English novel, and with the religious sense went the sense of the importance of the human act. It was as if the world of fiction had lost a *dimension*.

Greene's novels restore that lost dimension. He began with experiments of the divided personality and the theme of betrayal in books like *The Man Within*, *The Name of Action* and *Rumour at Nightfall*. He went to the study of the crime acts in what he called *Entertainments—Stamboul Train* and *Confidential Agent*. But he soon emerged as a major Catholic novelist in his great works, *Brighton Rock*, *The Power and the Glory*, *The Heart of the Matter*, *The End of the Affair* and *The Burnt Out Case*. These novels show Greene as a major author, who, to use the words of Francois Mauriac, "broke like a burglar into the kingdom of nature and Grace". Greene as a religious writer has met with some disapproval from strict theologians; his novels nevertheless have about them a religious validity, for they are not totally unfounded on doctrine.

Greene concerned himself with the horror of life. He writes a murder, suicide, and every form of violence. But he has raised the despairing and shady side of life to a supreme work of art possessing the greatest of philosphical disquisitions and truths. To dark acts he adds the illumination derived from the institutional philosophy of Catholicism. In this he is in contrast to most of his contemporaries who are concerned with 'The dis-integration of culture and the degradation of man. . . not theological evil'.

Greene makes an exploration into God through theological evil. Pinkie in *Brighton Rock* is a youthful criminal sadist. He kills ruthlessly and goes even to the point of tutoring his wife to commit suicide. Nemesis overtakes him fast and he is fatally burnt with the vitriol with which he wanted to destroy his wife in case she hesitated to take her own life. Over all the insensate deeds and crimes in the story there rises transcendingly the mercy of God. Pinkie dies apparently in sin. Still the good priest whispers to his widow in the confessional: "You can't conceive, my child, nor can I or anyone. . . the appalling. . . strangeness of the mercy of God", and exhorts her to make the baby she is going to have a saint 'to pray for his father'.

In *The Power and the Glory,* set in Mexico during the religious persecution, a bad priest flees from the law into the jungle. He is an alcoholic who has abjured religion. Yet when the need arises he absolves other sinner and turns the wafer into the mystical body and blood of Christ. He is finally captured and condemned to death. Before his execution he crouches on the floor; his drained brandy flask in his hand, and prays brokenly : "O God, I am sorry for all my sins. . . worthy of thy dreadful punishment". The whisky priest becomes the martyr of the Church. In the sanctity of his irrevocable office as a priest and in his death are visible the power and the glory of God.

The same mystical processes are seen in *The Heart of the Matter*. Scobbie commits suicide, but Father Rank tells his widow : "The Church knows all the rules. But it doesn't know what goes on in a single human heart. . . . It may seem an odd thing to say—when a man's as wrong as he (Scobbie) was—but I think, from what I saw of him, that he really loved God". Scobbie is saved by God's mercy.

The *End of the Affair* set in London during the Blitz is the story of an adulterous love affair. Sarah prays for the safety of Bendrix her lover and falls in love with God as she had done with Bendrix. Sarah the slut becomes Sarah the saint, for sainthood is given even to corrupt human nature : "we have to be pushed around. We are inextricably bound to the plot, and wearily God forces us, here and there, according to his intention. . . ."

'*The Burnt Out Case*' is the story of a world famous architect who retires from his profession, retires from the world, retires from his mistress, and retires from his faith and seeks asylum in a leproseire in the heart of Africa. And yet it is of this man that Fr. Thomas says : "There are interior prayers, the prayers of silence. There are even unconscious prayers when men have goodwill. A thought from you may be a prayer in the eyes of God.

All these novels of Greene deal with some fundamental concepts of the Catholic faith. Man is given free will and he can elicit his own salvation or damnation. Our souls are sustained by grace which comes from God. Greene, however, does go into paradoxes not easily understandable. For instance in the '*Heart of the Matter*' he writes "Only the man of good will carries away in his heart the capacity for damnation!", or "How often lack of faith helps one to see more clearly than faith". These contradictions do not easily reconcile themselves. The morbid computations with cause damnation, sin and lack of faith, Greene transfers to the promotion of virtue, salvation and faith. Sin is a reality and it is the reality of sin which makes one realise the reality of virtue. All very paradoxical, but true. And thus the sordid story becomes a salvation study in *excelsis*.

Francois Mauriac, the great French novelist and winner of the Nobel Prize is another who discovers religion through base human motives such as despair and greed in '*The Knot of Vipers*' and hypocrisy in '*A Woman of the Pharisees*. But Mauriac does not accept religion as a hereditary gift for in such cases, he says, we are "inundated with light".

For Greene who says "It needed a God to die for the half-hearted and the corrupt", it is not merely a Hound of Heaven story of a God pursuing a fleeing soul, but the conquest by God of a challenging and defiant sinner who stands his ground. Perhaps true—not for these people normally situated in life, but those abnormally placed as in nearly all modern *fiction driven by sin and despair.*

Greene anneals by his art, not just "realism and spirituality but institutional Catholicism and a personal philosophy of God, mercy and sanctifying grace. This is the new variant he gives to religion and within it recovers, in a traditional and yet individual way, the mission of the lost dimension in the form of the modern novel indulged by contemporary "emotional onanists".

The human race is involved in some terrible calamity and lives in an atmosphere of hatred and fear, but it is not without the hope of salvation. The modern realistic novel can be a means to the presentation of an idealism arising *out of the* lives who mussed it all their life. The modern realistic novel has a great future if it will only hold on to positive, definite and definitive truths (the lost dimension) as Graham Greene does, and refrain from spending itself in negations and only portraying to the exclusion of everything else, the dreadful urgencies, the shames and the crimes of mankind.

16

Tension in Poetry and Shakespeare's The Phoenix and the Turtle

This research paper has been provoked by a critical situation caused by three factors: the first is F.R. Leavis's taste and judgment in *New Bearings in English Poetry* later confirmed in 1950 when he appended the chapter 'Retrospect' to his book published twenty years earlier, the second is L.C. Knights's analysis of "Upon Westminster Bridge" in the Times Literary Supplement in July 26, 1963, and the third is the new criticism of A. Alvarez on "The Phoenix and the Turtle" in *Interpretations* edited by John Wain. Each of these, as criticism generally does, works within a limited field of operation, and in so doing raises questions on fundamentals, e.g. the nature of poetry and the kind of conceptual clarity and theoretical awareness which a critic should possess. By taking Shakespeare's "The Phoenix and the Turtle' as the basis for the study and analysing it in relation to that important constituent of poetry, namely, tension, one would inevitably modify or reconstitute in a measure the poetic criteria used by the scholar-critics, F.R. Leavis, L.C. Knights and A. Alvarez. The critical venture and that with Shakespeare's complex poem of many meanings and techniques is offered as a humble tribute to Shakespeare in the Quatercentenary year of his birth in 1964.

When F.R. Leavis wrote *New Bearings in English poetry* in the 'thirties one of his main objects was to revitalize poetry with greater strength and subtlety than what the Victorians could accomplish. He sampled extracts from William Empson and Ronald Bottrall—verses highly intellectualized. The romantic tradition of 'imaginative lucidity' gave way to 'logical perspicuity' which came the hard way, for the reader had to overcome a good deal of stubborn and resistant material in the diction, tropes and imagery used by the poets. Despite all this, one finds kinship with the configuration of the images and the significance of the poet's perception of the order of reality in the twentieth century. The intellectual element in poetry is not the major point but, as I submit a certain expressed tension arising out of disintegration and crisis either in the age or in the poet himself or in the materials he handles.

Ronald Bottrall in *The Future is Not for Us* describes this break-up of values or tension in the age :

'We are dismembered
Into a myriad broken shadows,
Each to himself reflected in a splinter of that glass
Which we once knew as cosmos, and the close
Of our long progress is hinted by the crass
Fogs creeping slowly and darkly
From out the middle West . . . . . . '

T.S. Eliot's *Gerontion* is another poem which besides dealing with the personal plight of a soul without ends and beatitudes is an historical poem of the age. Gerontion thinks of history significantly in relation to an annihilating or annihilated social order[1]:

'Think now
History has many cunning passages, contrived corridors
And issues, deceives with whispering ambitions,
Guides us by vanities'.

This trend of observing the tension in the age expressed in poetry constitutes an important element for critical evaluation or the writing of any History of English Literature as adumbrated by James Reeves.[2]

A poem besides being involved in the flux of historical time, has a separate independent or 'extra-historical existence.'[3] The poem is a composite, whole and entire, with an independent life of its own. It expresses a condition of tension in the opposite thoughts and feelings, images and rhythms, employed by the poet and which eventually indicate the tension within the poet. L.C. Knights works this out in his analysis of Wordsworth's sonnet "Upon Westminster Bridge," Sept. 3, 1802. He finds in it a fusion of opposites : the vulnerable and the awesome invulnerable :

> 'feelings and attitudes springing from our experience of what is young and vulnerable, that we should like to protect, fuse with our sense of things towards which we feel awe, in respect of which we who are young, inexperienced or powerless'.

and further on :

> 'the buildings momentarily appear as right—as proportioned, inviting and composed—as nature's valleys and hills; the old shackled city ("Near where the charter'd Thames does flow") is as the morning. There is no self-deception : beauty that is "like a garment" can, we know be put off; the "smokeless air" will soon be smoke-filled and the supreme quiet contains the pulse of life about to resume its course'.[4]

But this sonnet or any romantic poem for that matter (barring Shelly's Triumph of life) is a fairly simple and partial situation to illustrate tension as a mere pull of opposites. The sonnet is concerned, as all Romantic poetry, mainly with the poet's feelings : the intellect plays no striking part in the expression of the tension or as Cleanth Brooks states : 'The Romantic poet distrusted the intellects as inimical to emotion and destructive of spontaneity.'[5]

If the intellect functions, as it ought to, the result is that the disparates in the poem are several and wide, the contrasts are sharp and striking, and the fusion is done at a high pitch of released emotion and logical thought. The total effect of all these is a poem inhered with complex tension and because of this, of a very high order.

A poem of this high quality or complex tension is Shakespeare's 'The Phoenix and the Turtle'. This poem was first published in Robert Chester's anthology *Loves Martyr*, 1601. It is in two parts : the main poem of 13 stanzas and a Threnos of 5 stanzas. The poem is at two levels—human and mystical. On the one hand it can be interpreted as a poem of human lovein passion or fulfilment or a human situation as A. Alvarez submits in *Interpretations.*[6] On the other, it is a poem mystical, transcendental and even religious. Stanza 9 of the poem describes the romantic and consuming fire of human love ;

'So between them loue did shine,
That the Turtle saw his right,
Flaming in the Phoenix sight;
Either was the others mine'.

The flame or fire image is like Donne's :

'. . . as one glorious flame
Meeting Another, growes the same'. (Epithalamion
. . . on the Lady Elizabeth, and Court Palatine)

In stanza 12 we have not just mere mating in wedlock but a kind of an 'Epipsychidion', a call of soul to soul or a fusion of souls :

'That it cried, how true a twaine,
Seemeth this concordant one,
Loue hath Reason, Reason none,
If what parts, can so remaine'.

The Phoenix and the Dove are, as stanze 13 states, 'Co-supremes and startes of love' which can be rendered in terms of medieval symbolism where the Phoenix stands for Christ and the dove for the soul seeking marriage with Christ :

> 'Leauing no posteritie,
> Twas not their infirmitie,
> It was married Chastitie.'

This is the kind of mystical experience and apprehension found in the writings of St. Therese of Lisieux where Christ is conceptualized as 'the bridgroom of the soul'. Such single interpretations of Shakespeare's poem aid the understanding of this difficult poem, but they in no way explain the organic unity or the organization of the poem which affords such dismemberment.

The whole poem can be unbuckled or evaluated at the level of the tension or the contradictions within it. This was the prevalent manner of Donne as in these lines:

> 'Our two soules therefore, which are one,
> Though I must goe, endure not yet
> A breach, but an expansion,
> Like gold to aiery thinnesse beat'.

Here the unity of the souls of the lovers is 'a non-spatial entity' which is conjoined to the opposite, a "spatial image" like the beaten or malleable gold.[7] The very separateness of the disparates and their diversified polarities brought together in clever ingenuity intensify the meaning so that the comparison or the collocation of the opposites, like in Metaphysical Poetry, is the vision of the poet or the crux of the poem in a structural sense.

In Shakespeare's poem there is the combination of contradictions. There are first the birds : the phoenix, the crow, and the dove; then there are the abstracts Love and Constancie, Beautie, Truth and Raritie ; and finally the lovers. All these three separate categories are wrought together and given an imaginative unity, the only kind of unity which matters in poetry. Take for example, stanze 6 where the abstracts and the birds and the union of spirits are brought together in effective coherence :

> 'Here the Antheme doth commence,
> Love and Constancie is dead,
> Phoenix and the Turtle fled
> In a mutuall flame from hence'.

The amalgamation of these diverse elements is done with great intellectual dexterity mingled with an equal measure of emotion in the fire imagery and the romantic view of lovers fled into the night in the ending of Keats's 'The Eve of St. Agnes'. Throughout this poem whether in its organic unity or its several parts there is the same bringing together of contraries. The opposites can be near one another in single lines or adjacent lines or deployed wide apart demanding sustained concentration and comprehension by the reader, as 'the bird of lowdest lay' in stanza 1 asked to 'sigh a prayer' in the last line of stanza 18. The poem is replete with near-juxtaposed opposites in idea, image and rhythm. In stanza 1 the idea of death and resurrection is given in the mingling of the sad and the joyous : 'Herald sad and trumpet be'. In stanza 3 there are contrasting images of predatory birds and the exalted 'windhover' :

> 'Every foule of tyrant wing,
> Saue the Eagle feathered King'.

In stanza 5 there is a complex of ryhthms, Sprung and Common: the first line has an accumulation of stresses and runs to speed like in Sprung Rhythm :

> 'And thou treble dated Crow':

the third line has an anapaest followed by two iambs in Common Rhythm :

> With the breath thou Giu'st and tak'st' makes the crow's caw or the sensuous mingle with the semantic in the words 'thou giu'st' and tak'st'.

Stanza 8 is an excellent one to illustrate how intellectualized concepts of contraries, following one upon another in quick succession, can be charged with passion and even romantic emotion :

> 'Hearts remote, yet not asunder;
> Distance and no space was seene,
> Twixt this Turtle and his Queene :
> But in them it were a wonder'.

In stanza 10, with extraordinary adroitness, there is a concept of form and matter as in Thomistic philosophy where the particularity or form exists in the matter and cannot be separated from it ; but this is given in a kind of "reductio ad absurdum" arising out of the perception of a tension in Nature :

> 'Properttie was thus appalled,
> That the selfe was not the same'.

Here the selfhood or the essence of form of the one bird is merged into matter, along with the selfhood or the essence of the other bird in the same unit of matter all in an alarming contrariness. The poet expatiates on this further in the next stanza :

> 'Reason in it selfe confounded,
> Saw Diuision grow together,
> To themselves yet either neither,
> Simple were so well compounded'.

The story of this love of birds or be it of mortals or of souls, takes on an allegorical significance in death in the first stanza {the Threnos :

> 'Beautie, Truth and Raritie,
> Grace in all simplicite,
> Here enclosde, in cinders lie'.

There is transcendence in love beyond Time and Space:

'Death is now the Phoenix nest,
And the Turtles loyall brest,
To eternities doth rest'. (Stanza 15)

The birds are dead and so the poet exhorts :

'To this vrne lest those repaire,
That are either true or faire'. (Stanza 18)

The birds or the Christ-soul relationship or the souls they symbolize have gained a new sainthood and so their mortal remains become a relic or an object for veneration and pilgrimage. The religious allegory is thus closed at the end, earlier begun in stanza 4 with 'the Priest in Surples white' and 'the Requiem'.

The Phoenix and the Turtle thus is a poem of great vitality and subtlety, complex and contradictory in its every part and cogently unified into a central meaning through both the structure and the texture of the poem or its extension and intension. Idea impinges on idea, feeling on feeling, idea on feeling and the reverse too, and all in a brilliant and fascinating continuum. In contrast Wordsworth's "Upon Westminster Bridge" is limited as an exposition of tension for he is primarily concerned with an attenuated aspect or the opposition *of elementary feeling to elementary feeling as embodied* in the city and Nature dichotomy or the memory of it.

The quality of the creative imagination and the measure of its strength lies in the complexity of its functions as it deals with tension; the way it combines the intellectual and the emotional, the objective and the experiential, the subtle and the simple or, as Allen Tate writes, all the devices used by the poet '*to push his meanings as far as he can towards the opposite* and so as to occupy the entire scale.'[8] Shakespeare did all this in "The Phoenix and the Turtle". He is still a living writer, surprisingly connected with the particularity of our age and modern poetry, the predominant note of which is 'a sense of conflict or tension.'[9] The expression of tension in his poem under review is vitally done in the images, the antithesis and *opposites used and resolved by him* as W.B. *Yeats does in*

"Byzantium" as a whole with 'its system of tensions'[10] or in the climacteric of the poem: 'That dolphin-torn, that gong-tormented sea' which combines love and despair, sex and religion, legend and reality.

REFERENCES

1. Lawrence Durrell, *Key to Modern Poetry* (Calcutta, 1961), p. 11.
2. James Reeves, *A Short History of English Poetry,* 1340-1940, (London 1961), p. XVI.
3. Ibid., p. XV.
4. The Times Literary Supplement, July 26, 1963: *In Search of Fundamental Values*, by L.C. Knights, p. 569.
5. Cleanth Brooks, *Modern Poetry and the Tradition* (London, 1948), p. 229.
6. Ed. John Wain, Interpretations (London, 1955), p. 9.
7. Allen Tate, The Man of Letters in the Modern World (New York, 1955), p. 72.
8. Ibid.
9. R.A. Foakes, The Romantic Assertion (London, 1958), p. 15.
10. T.R. Henn, The Lonely Tower (London, 1950), pp. 215 and 223.

17

Poetic Diction

It is plain that poetry is distinguished from prose in as much as the two are different ways of expression of the human mind. We cannot say that poetry makes use of a vocabulary altogether different from that of prose. Words are common in both. The difference lies in the use of words rather than words as such. That brings us to a distinction between the diction of poetry and the diction of prose. This distinction is nothing but one of peculiarity in the use of words in the two fields of literature. Secondly we can argue that poetry occupies a region above prose. It is of course true that prose in its highest flights approaches the plane of poetry and poetry in its lowest descent draws near the level of prose. But they are yet essentially different. This truth is brought out clearly when we compare the same fact or incident of history as related in poetry and prose. As for example, the "Aeneid" is very unlike a prose account of the founding of Rome.

Wordsworth once wrote to one of the critics of his "Idiot boy"—It is probably that the principal case of your dislike to the particular poem lies in the word 'idiot'. If there had been any such word in our language to which we had attached passion, as lack wit, half wit, witless etc., I should have certainly empolyed it in preference, but there is no such word.

Wordsworth here perhaps finds some sort of difficulty with the word 'idiot'. The difficulty, however, lies in no single word as John Livingston Lowes would point out, certainly not in 'idiot'. If we compare Wordsworth with Shakesphare, we find there is absolutely nothing wrong with the word itself.

> "Why bustle thou about your door,
> What means this bustle
> Why are your
> And why
> Him".

and in Shakespeare:

> "......... . it is a tale
> told by an idiot, full of sound and fury
> signifying nothing".

As Sir Walter Raliegh pointed out, poets redeem words from degradation by a single noble employment! Shakespeare has saved 'idiot' if it required salvation and the wrong with W. was that his employment of the word is not noble. Words in themselves are neither poetic nor unpoetic. 'They become poetic' as Lowes has pointed out, or they remain unassimilated prose according as the poet's imaginative energy is or is not, sufficiently powerful to absorb them.

The use of words in prose and poetry thus shall differ according to the different functions that they have. In other words, the diction of poetry and that of prose depends upon a difference between the function of words in the two mediums. The business of words in prose is primarily to state and in poetry the business is not only to state but also to suggest. "Words have an emotional and imaginative as well as an intellectual context. The last is the chief determining factor in prose and it is the first which powerfully operates in poetry". But we cannot create poetry merely collecting a group of the so called poetic words in common prose use. As a matter of fact, words which are apparently so prasaic and unimaginative have contributed to such magnificent diction in poetry with poets of real power and vigour. In famous and often quoted lines like—

'Come the mortal wretch
with thy sharp teath this knot intrinsicate
of life at once unite'.

or in 'The multitudinous seas incardine'

Macbeth

or in 'She is in her grave and Oh
the difference to me'

Lucy

We find apparently unpoetic words like intrinsicate, multitudinous, incardine and difference etc. give such brilliant imaginative *associations and such wonderful poetic effect*. So at the outset there should be no illusion with regard to poetic diction that it consists in certain choice words and choice epithets. Words in general are the material out of which the poetry builds his edifice of poetry. No matter what words they are, it depends on the poet in what way he makes use of them. The use of words in poetry in other words the diction of poetry will differ from that of prose from no other reason *but that the function of poetry differs from that of prose*. By a simple analogy how the diction of poetry can be distinguished from that of prose it is like a temple of bricks and mortar distinguished from a house of the dame material. Here, it should not be thought that often ordinary buildings are used to instal gods, as much as prose forms are *often used to write* poetry. Because in discussing the diction of poetry we leave aside the consideration of all those poetic prose or prose-*poetry*.

The chief illusion thus being cleared, it remains to set a few more points pertinent to the question. When we establish that the poet's vocabulary is not different from that of prose writer what happens to poetry in general. Should it be always as *Wordsworth enunciated, identical with the* language of prose or should it be a selection of language really used by men? It is in fact the right of the poet to create his own language. It is ipso facto a outcome of his own mind. We agree with Horace when he says that wide discretion should be exercised in the choice of words. Therefore, as Eliot points out, the immediacy of poetry to conversation is not a matter on which we can lay down exact laws. Every resolution in poetry is apt to be and sometimes to announce itself as a return to common speech. But we don't want the poet to merely reproduce exactly the conversational medium of himself, his family, his friends and his particular district, but what he finds there is the material out of which he must make his poetry. He must, like the sculpture, be faithful to the medium in which he works, it is out of sounds that he must make his melody and harmony. The poet has his particular choice not imposed from outside but from himself. He is the creator of his own language. If a picture will be a piece of poem, the colour will be its diction. This colour is selected by the artist himself. So the poet while creating poetry, automatically creates his diction.

So finally, we must arrive at the conclusion that there is no language which is called poetic diction. It becomes superb due to the ennobling influence of poetry. As John Livingstone Lowes said 'it is poetry, which through its emerging influence, gives to words poetic quality, it is not poetic diction which makes poetry.

18

Tension in Poetry

When F.R. Leavis wrote *New Bearings in English Poetry* in the 'Thirties one of his main objects was to revitalize poetry with greater strength and subtlety than what the Victorians could accomplish. He sampled extracts from William Empson and Ronald Bottrall—verses highly intellectualized. The romantic tradition of 'imaginative lucidity' gave way to 'logical perspicuity' which came the hard way, for the reader had to overcome a good deal of stubborn and resistant material in the diction, tropes and imagery used by the poets. Despite all this, one finds kinship with the configuration of the images and the significance of the poet's perception of the order of reality in the twentieth century. The intellectual element in poetry is not the major point but, as I submit in this paper, a certain expressed tension arising out of disintegration and crisis either in the age or in the poet himself or in the materials he handles.

Ronald Bottrall in *The Future is Not for Us* describes this break-up of values or tension in the age :

> 'We are dismembered
> Into a myriad broken shadows,
> Each to himself reflected in a splinter of that glass
> Which we once knew as cosmos, and the close

of our long progress is hinted by the crass
Fogs creeping slowly and darkly
From out the middly West. . .'

T.S. Eliot's *Gerontion* is another poem which besides dealing with the personal plight of a soul without ends and beatitudes is an historical poem of the age. Gerontion thinks of history significantly in relation to an annihilating or annihilated social order[1] :

> 'Think now
> History has many cunning passages, contrived corridors
> And issues, deceives with whispering ambitions,
> Guides us by vanities'.

This trend of observing the tension in the age expressed in poetry constitutes an important element for critical evaluation or the writing of any History of English Literature as adumbrated by James Reeves.[2]

A poem besides being involved in the flux of historical time, has a separate independent or 'extra historical existence'.[3] The poem is a composite, whole and entire, with an independent life of its own. It expresses a condition of tension in the opposite thoughts and feelings, images and rhythms, employed by the poet and which eventually indicate the tension within the poet. L.C. Knights works this out in his analysis of Wordsworth's sonnet *Upon Westminster Bridge*, Sept. 3, 1802. He finds in it a fusion of opposites : the vulnerable and the awesome invulnerable :

> 'feelings and attitudes springing from our experience of what is young and vulnerable, that we should like to protect, fuse with our sense of things towards which we feel awe, in respect of which we who are young, inexperienced or powerless.'

and further on :

> 'the buildings momentarily appear as right—as proportioned, inviting and composed—as nature's valleys and

> hills; the old shackled city ("Near where the charter'd Thames does flow") is as the morning. There is no self-deception : beauty that is "like a garment" can, we know, be put off; the "smokeless air" will soon be smoke-filled; and the supreme quiet contains the pulse of life about to resume its course'.[4]

But this sonnet or any romantic poem for that matter (barring Shelley's Triumph of Life) is a fairly simple and partial situation to illustrate tension as a mere pull of opposites. The sonnet is concerned, as all Romantic poetry, mainly with the poet's feelings : the intellect plays no striking part in the expression of the tension or as Cleanth Brooks states : 'The Romantic poet distrusted the intellect as inimical to emotion and destructive of spontaneity.'[5]

If the intellect functions, as it ought to, the result is that the disparates in the poem are several and wide, the contrasts are sharp and striking, and the fusion is done at a high pitch of released emotion and logical thought. The total effect of all these is a poem inhered with complex tension and because of this, of a very high order.

A poem of this high quality or complex tension is Shakespeare's *The Phoenix and the Turtle*. This poem was first published in Robert Chester's anthology *Loves Martyr*, 1901. It is in two parts : the main poem of 13 stanzas and a Threnos of 5 stanzas. The poem is at two levels—human and mystical. On the one hand it can be interpreted as a poem of human love in passion or fulfilment or a human situation as A. Alvarez submits in *Interpretations*.[6] On the other, it is a poem mystical, transcendental and even religious. Stanza 9 of the poem describes the romantic and consuming fire of human love :

> 'So between them loue did shine,
> That the Turtle saw his right,
> Flaming in the *Phoenix* sight;
> Either was the others mine.'

The flame or fire image is like Donne's :

'. . . as one glorious flame
Meeting Another, growes the same '(*Epithalamion*'
on the Lady Elizabeth, and Count Palatine)

In stanza 12 we have not just mere mating in wedlock but a kind of an *Epipsychidion*, a call of soul to soul or a fusion of souls :

'That it cried, how true a twaine,
Seemeth this concordant one,
Loue hath Reason, Reason none,
If what parts, can so remaine'.

The Phoenix and the Dove are, as stanza 13 states, 'Co-supremes and startes of love' which can be rendered in terms of medieval symbolism where the Phoenix stands for Christ and the dove for the soul seeking marriage with Christ :

'Leauing no posteritie,
Twas not their infirmitie,
It was married Chastitie'.

This is the kind of mystical experience and apprehension found in the writings of St. Therese of Lisieux where Christ is conceptualized as 'the bridegroom of the soul'. Such single interpretations of Shakespeare's poem aid the understanding of this difficult poem, but they in no way explain the organization of the poem which affords such dismemberment.

The whole poem can be unbuckled or evaluated at the level of the tension or the contradictions within it. This was a prevalent manner of Donne as in these lines :

'Our two soules therefore, which are one,
Though I must goe, endure not yet
A breach, but an expansion,
Like gold to aiery thinnesse beat'.

Here the unity of the souls of the lovers is "a *non-spatial entity*" which is conjoined to the opposite, a "spatial image" like the beaten or malleable gold.[7] The very separateness of the disparates and their diversified polarities brought together in clever ingenuity intensify the meaning so that the comparison or the collocation of the opposites, like in Metaphysical Poetry, is the vision of the poet or the crux of the poem in a structual sense.

In Shakespeare's poem there is the combination of contradictions. There are first the birds : the phoenix, the crow, and the dove; then there are the abstracts Love and Constancie, Beautie, Truth and Raritie; and finally the lovers. All these three separate categories are wrought together and given an imaginative unity, the only kind of unity which matters in poetry. Take for example, stanza 6 where the abstracts and the birds and the union of spirits are brought together in effective coherence :

'Here the Antheme doth commence,
Love and Constancie is dead,
Phoenix and the *Turtle* fled
In a mutuall flame from hence'.

The amalgamation of these diverse elements is done with great intellectual dexterity mingled with an equal measure of emotion in the fire imagery and the romantic view of lovers fled into the night in the ending of Keats's *The Eve of St. Agnes*. Throughout this poem whether in its organic unity or its several parts there is the same bringing together of contraries. The opposites can be near one another in single lines or adjacent lines or deployed wide apart demanding sustained concentration and comprehension by the reader, as 'the bird of lowdest lay' in stanza 1 asked to 'sigh a prayer' in the last line of stanza 18. The poem is replete with near-juxtaposed opposites in idea, image and rhythm. In stanza 1 the idea of death and resurrection is given in the mingling of the sad and the joyous: 'Herald sad and trumpet be'. In stanza 3 there are contrasting images of predatory birds and the exalted 'windhover' :

'Euery foule of tyrant wing,
Saue the Eagle feath'red King'.

In stanza 5 there is a complex of rhythms, sprung and common : first line has an accumulation of stresses and runs to speed like in Sprung Rhythm :

'And thou treble dated Crow';

the third line has a number of unstressed syllables followed by two stresses in 'giu'st' and 'tak'st'. The presence of these words in the line 'With the breath thou Giu'st and tak'st makes the Crow's caw, or the sensuous mingle with the semantic in a forward and backward movement as in Donne's *Elegy XII* :

'Since she must go, and I must mourn'.

Stanza 8 is an excellent one to illustrate how intellectualized concepts of contraries, following one upon another in quick succession, can be charged with passion and even romantic emotion :

'Hearts remote, yet not asunder;
Distance and no space was seene,
'Twixt this *Turtle* and his Queene;
But in them it were a wonder'.

In stanza 10, with extraordinary adroitness, there is a concept of form and matter as in Thomistic philosophy where the particularity or form exists in the matter and cannot be separated from it; but this is given in a kind of *reductio ad absurdum* arising out of the perception of a tension in Nature :

'Properttie was thus appalled,
That the selfe was not the same'.

Here the selfhood of the essence of form of the one bird is merged into matter, along with the selfhood or the essence of the other bird in the same unit of matter all in an alarming contrariness. The poet expatiates on this further in the next stanza :

'Reason in it selfe confounded,
Saw Diuision grow together,
To themselves yet either neither,
Simple were so well compounded'.

The story of this love of birds or be it of mortals or of souls, takes on an allegorical significance in death in the first stanza of the Threnos :

'Beautie, Truth, and Raritie,
Grace in all simplicitie,
Here enclosde, in cinders lie'.

There is transcendence in love beyond Time and Space :

'Death is now the *Phoenix* nest,
And the Turtles loyall brest,
to eternities doth rest'. (Stanza 15)

The birds are dead and so the poet exhorts :
'To this vrne lest those repaire,
That are either true or faire'.
(Stanza 18)

The birds or the Christ-soul relationship or the souls they symolize have gained a new sainthood and so their mortal remains become a relic or an object for veneration and pilgrimage. The religious allegory is thus closed at the end, earlier begun in stanza 4 with 'the Priest in Surples white' and 'the Requiem'.

The Phoenix and the Turtle thus is a poem of great vitality and subtlety, complex and contradictory in its every part and cogently unified into a central meaning through both the structure and the texture of the poem or its extension and intention. Idea impinges on idea, feeling on feeling, idea on feeling and the reverse too, and all in a brilliant and fascinating continuum. In contrast Wordsworth's *Upon Westminster Bridge* is limited as an exposition of tension for he is primarily concerned with an attenuated aspect or the opposition of elementary feeling to elementary feeling as embodied in the city and Nature or the memory of it. The quality of the creative imagination and the measure of its strength lies in the complexity of its functions as it deals with tension : the way it combines the intellectual and the emotional, the objective and the experiential, the subtle and the simple or, as Attel Tate writes, all the devices used by the poet 'to push his meanings as far as he can towards the opposite end so as to occupy the entire scale.'[7]

REFERENCES

1. Lawrence Durrell: *Key to Modern Poetry*, (1961), p. 11.
2. James Reeves: *A Short History of English Poetry*, (1961), p. XVI.
3. *Ibid.*, p. XV.
4. *The Times Literary Supplement*, July 26, 1963: 'In Search of Fundamental Values' by L.C. Knights, p. 569.
5. Cleanth Brooks: Modern Poetry and the Tradition, (1948), p. 229.
6. Ed. John Wain: Interpretations, (1955), p. 9.
7. Allen Tate: *The Man of Letters in the Modern World*, (1955), p. 72.

19

Singular Minds and Love Letters: D.H. Lawrence

D.H. Lawrence, the novelist and poet, is one of the most controversial figures in twentieth century literature. He was born in 1885 and died in 1930 barely forty four years old. He was a strange and peculiar character who had a concept of life and art which brought him much misery when he was alive, and ranged critics into two camps, for and against him. This strange, obscure and occult writer has been much abused. He was condemned for what was taken as vulgar and prurient literature. The writer, Melville, describes him as 'clownish and sententiously bad in taste'; the critic of the novel, Dorothy M. Hoare, found 'a sadistic element' in all he wrote; Middleton Murry essayed on a destructive attack of the Lawrence hagiorgraphy in *Son of Woman*. Richard Aldington called him a genius and while admitting that, in his *Portrait of a Genius*, pointed to the 'mass of obscenity of thought, idea, and action' in this lone and isolated character who lived as he died, unconnected to society—forlorn and forsaken. Gradually, the facts of his life were separated from his work, and a new approach brought to light the essential genius of the writer.

Aldous Huxley found him 'different and superior in kind' to any one in twentieth century literature. E.M. Forster called him 'the greatest imaginative writer of our age'. F.R. Leavis evaluated him as a great and sensitive literary artist and, in his book, *The Great Tradition*, mentions him as having brought to us a new awareness of our being and the possibilities of life.

Whatever critics or people may say, it is good to face this challenging writer oneself. The adventure is worthwhile and the result may prove fruitful. We have his great novels like *The White Peacock*, *Aaron's Rod*, *Kangaroo*, *The Plumed Serpent*, *Women in Love*, *The Rainbow*, *Lady Chatterley's Lover* and his manum opus, *Sons and Lovers*. In addition to all this, we have his *Collected Poems*, his last philosophical book, *Apocalypse*, and a large volume of letters covering 853 printed pages edited by Aldous Huxley and other letters found in Frieda Lawrence's book *Not I but the Wind* and other collections, such as, that by Harry T. Moore. Lawrence was a prolific correspondent and his letters actually laid bare his soul and his mind and all those perturbations, aching joys and smarting pains, hardships, hopes and disillusionments, which were so much a part of his short life. The letters too indicate the positive criteria of his thinking and his passionate vision. The letters were written to Frieda Lawrence, the mother of three children, and the wife of Ernest Weekley, one of his former professors at Nottingham; he eloped with her and completely identified her with his whole being. This is part of the story of *The Savage Pilgrimage* recorded by Catherine Carswell with the greatest sympathy and in vicious attack of Middleton Murry's carping book, *Son of Woman*. Murry actually went to Law over Catherine Carswell's book till the offensive statements about him were finally expurgated from the edition. The Frieda-Lawrence story makes shocking reading from every normal standard of decency and good conduct; but then,—*that* life left its mark on what Lawrence created and communicated in much of his writings, so that it seems, at all events, that such an experience was an impelling necessity for the author. There are several letters, besides, addressed to friends and acquaintances like David and Edward

Garnett, A.W. McLeod, Ernest Collings, Aldous Huxley, and women like Catherine Carswell, Lady Ottoline Morrell, Hon. Dorothy Brett and Katherine Mansfield. Most of these letters were self-explanations of his life, his strange ego, and his aims and objects as an artist.

At the outset Lawrence looked upon Sex as phallic and religious. As a sensitive child his attachment to his mother had, as he later described it, an Oedipus Complex. This relation finds autobiographical expression in *Sons and Lovers*. With his mother's death ended an era of this unusual mother-son relation. With the coming of Frieda he at last came into the keeping and possession of a woman, other than his mother. In both these phases of his life, with and without his mother, there is the same awe and ecstasy of sex, which he believed gives mystery to life and a personal religion to an individual. Of Woman, he wrote to Edward Garnett, in rather blasphemous terms: 'And God the Father, the Inscrutable, the Unknowable, we know in the Flesh, in Woman...' He regarded woman as the eternal continuance who provoked in man a 'new self-revelation'. This view of Woman, conceived very early in his life, was affirmed by his affair with Frieda. Referring to his honeymoon, he wrote to Mrs. S.A. Hopkin, 'Life can be great quite Sod-like. It *can* be so. God be thanked I have proved it. 'He wrote to Frieda, times without number, that he loved her. 'He understood the anti-social character of his attachment and wrote with unconcealed distress: 'I feel so horried and helpless. I know it all sicknes you'...and that although 'I love you—Lord I pay for it'.

Frieda appears an inevitable corroboration and conviction of the view he all along conceived in his novels. He wrote to Lady Ottiline Morrell in 1928: 'You will understand what I'm trying to do the full natural rapprochment of a man and a woman: and the re-entry into life of a bit of the old phallic awareness and the old phallic insouciance'. Readers of his works hardly consider his view-point. Katherine Mansfield, for instance, was filled with repugnance for him. Lawrence wrote to her in self-defence: 'Frieda said. . . I repulsed you' and that not Jung or Freud motivated him, but a flash of inspiration—'It was a star that blazed for a second in one's soul'.

Inevitably Lawrence put a premium on the body with all its sensations. He built up this concept. 'My great religion', he wrote, 'is a belief in the blood, the flesh, as being wiser than the intellect...' and what the blood feels, and believes, and says, is always true.' He followed this up with a letter to Edward Garnett: 'Somehow, that which is physic-non-human in humanity, is more interesting to me than the old-fashioned human element, which causes one to conceive a character in a certain moral scheme'. He contrasts himself with Turgenev, Tolstoy and Dostoievsky and other writers with moral schemes. He has no cosmic vision of life, such as, Thomas Mann in his novel, *The Magic Mountain* or Eugene O' Neill in his play, *Strange Interlude*.

Lawrence claimed to have apprehended reality or 'the dark presence of otherness' as Aldous Huxley describes it. He went beyond the boundaries of man's consciousness into the dark regions of the unconscious where man's ego lies submerged. He regarded sex as 'the immediate, non-mental knowledge of divine otherness'. F.R. Leavis finds him a visionary like Blake as he could distinguish between feeling and conventional sentiment. Art existed in a complex personal experience or as Lawrence wrote to Ernest Collings: 'Art for my sake...If I want to write, I write—'. Thus was transferred to the novel the discoveries of his creation got by his sheer intuition and inspiration. He wrote from the depths of his own being, so that a book, like *Lady Chatterley's Lover*, is at bottom, the author's life as is *Sons and Lovers*. Lawrence travelled much in Europe, Mexico, Australia, and even India. All this outward world of men did not attract or give him a social ego. He abjured England, with a Byronic contempt. He wrote to A.W. McLeod: 'I want to wash again quitely, wash off England, the oldness and grubbiness and despair'. He took refuge in himself and that sanctity. To Edward Garnett, he unveils himself: 'Primarily I am a passionately religious man, and my novels must be written from the depth of my religious experience'.

There is something primitive and pathetic about all this confusion of religion and life, the obsolute and the relative. What Lawrence lacks is a sharp critical faculty. He was a man of profound insights but he lacked the powers of argument and ratiocination. T.S. Eliot found him contrary to tradition and free from all institutions. This island life in which he lived did produce burning literature, but hardly living literature as we understand it in the individual or collective sense. As we pass from one book of his to another, he appears—as Richard Aldington describes the symptoms of our experience—'winding, tedious and nauseating'. He was trying to say just one thing all his life. He was flimsily and exigously related to the world we live in. He wrote of sexual matters because he found that life was encrusted with an excess of intellectualization. But then to divest life of all intellectualization is another extreme. God cannot be, as Lawrence posited, only 'a vast shimmering impulse'. The purblindness to the nature of God and society, were his misfortune, and although he gives us a world of art, it is a world detached from the wise restraints of philosophy, ethics and religion in the theological sense, all of which have their purpose in life. Without them life is just drift; with them, a definite course leading to a definite end.

20

American Literature and Indians

Indians who take up the study of American literature will find a theme with which they are quite familiar : the essential oneness and indivisibility of all life. This American Vedantism, especially in and after the days of Emerson and Thoreau, owes much to India. It is truly Oriential thought in Western garb though there are certain differences, due to the adaptation of Advaita to American needs and conditions. From the beginning Americans, like some Indians in later times, believed that the life force dwelling in all phenomena. the Brahman, being one, literally equalizes all men socially and politically as well as cosmically and makes them not only parts one of another but equivalent parts. Americans have also tended to believe that the doctrine of Brahman, of the All-One, makes each responsible for all and social service the chief activity, perhaps, through which what is divine man can express itself. It is interesting to note that it was from America, in the 1890's, that Swami Vivekananda wrote burning letters to his brother monks urging them to believe that God, being "the sum total of all souls", required them to succour the wicked, the miserable, and the poor of all races and species. Since his time Karma Yoga has claimed the allegiance of some of the greatest Indians, such as Gandhi, Aurobindo, and Bhave, but never has it been interpreted by them in quite the simple, literal, social service sense common in America. This may be a defect in American Vedantism but surely the defect of an excellence.

Emerson's doctrine of the Oversoul is simply that of Brahman animating every conceivable thing which we call alive and extending even to stocks and stones. In this Brahman, "Aboriginal Self", or "Oversoul", "the last fact behind which analysis cannot go", all things find their common origin, "for the sense of being which in calm hours rises, we know not how, in the soul is not diverse from things, from space, from life, from time, from man, but one with them and proceeds obviously from the same source whence their life and being also proceeds . . . . . We lie in the lap of immense intelligence which makes us receivers of its truth and organs of its activity". Most of Emerson's essays are attempts to subtilize the common conceptions of self-reliance, art, intellect, love, heroism, and fate as understood in America in his time by referring them to his concept of Brahman, which he called Over-soul—"the ultimate fact which we so quickly reach . . . . on every topic, the resolution of all into the over-blessed One". Everything from the pangs of conscience to the pleasures of gift-giving Emerson attributed to the fact that we are literally parts of one great Spirit, who hurt ourselves when we do wrong to others and gladden ourselves through every pleasure which we give them. All men everywhere are enmeshed in a great web whose filaments bind every mind everywhere on earth to every other mind. To be sure, this great network is invisible, but so are electrons, and the seed of life itself, as Svetaketu learned. Self-reliance, to Emerson, was not the conviction that if at first you do not succeed, try try again but trust in the great Trustee, who is essentially the composite urge to love and labour for love found in the whole human race. The truly self-reliant man stands, as it were, at the apex of a pyramid composed of mankind. His foot is, as Whitman wrote, "tenoned and mortised in granite". He cannot slip or fall because he is upheld by absolute, deathless love. Of course, the drive toward love and love-work—the assence of the Brahman or Self and the only source of profound experience—is not equally active in all human beings. In fact, it may be entirely dormant in some, driven into unconscious depths, as Emerson would say, by miseducation, bad family teaching, and the climate of a materialistic culture. It was the mission of the great Transcendentalists like Emerson, Thoreau, and Whitman to bring the repressed Brahman to the surface.

We should always remember of Thoreau that he went to Walden Pond not in order to escape from his obligations as a human being but in order to cleanse his spirit of the grit caused by association with those who act in ignorance of the true Self. This Self Thoreau found satisfactorily described in the books he took the Pond : the "Vedas", the "Bhagavat-Geeta". the Vishnu Purana, and the Harivansa. With the help of these books Thoreau could see easily, he said, to Tartary on one hand and to China on the other, that is, around the world, which is the irreducible theatre of the Oversoul. Communing with Eastern sages, every particle of unstoried dust at Walden revealed itself to Thoreau as part of the ancient "Brahma", and thus an otherwise lonely and tentative American joined his spirit with that of the whole human race, living and dead, in a mystic exaltation in which solitude was no longer "solitude, nor poverty poverty, nor weakness weakness". Such an experience, in which all the great "times and places and occasions" of the past are "now and here", in which "God Himself culminates in the present moment", is the combium point where the tree of life puts forth new leaves and makes sure of a broad-branched future. From such an experience, well known to the forest-sages of India, Thoreau returned "cleansed of grit" to the practice of love-in-society.

Such an experience, said Thoreau, is the typical object of every American's quest and the inspiration of America's greatest poetry, an assertion which Whitman did much to substantiate. Unlike the missionary in Forester's A Passage to India, who thought there might be a touch of divine life in the higher animals but could not bring himself to find it in wasps, oranges and mud, Whitman wrote :

> I find I incorporate gneiss, coal, long-threaded moss,
> fruits, grains, esculent roots,
> I am stucco'd with quadrupeds and birds all over. . . . .

In vain the snake slides through the creepers and logs,
In vain the elk takes to the inner passes of the wood,
In vain the razor-bill'd auk skils far north to Labrador,
I follow quickly, I ascend to the nest in the fissures of
the cliff.

In "Song of Myself" Whitman was concerned to distinguish the little, convulsive, egoistic self from what is truly divine in man :

My dinner, dress, associates, looks, compliments, views,
The real or fancied indifference of some man or woman
I love. . . . . . .
Battles, the horrors of fratricidal war, the fever of doubt-
ful news, the fitful events;
These come to me days and nights and go from me again,
Bet they are not the Me Myself.

Whitman conceived that men had never been happy since their separation at Babel and that it was his role as a poet to bring them together again in love and understanding, for

He who walk a furlong without sympathy
Goes to his grave wrapped in his own shroud.

He hailed the transcontinental railway and the Suez Canal, completed in the same year, as symbols of spiritual communication on an advaitic scale. Before the unpleasantness at the Tower of Babel all men had been alike in speech, complexion and understanding. Ever since Babel they had been miserable in the separation. But now they can return to the Edenic state.

Down from the gardens of Asia descending, radiating,
Adam and Eve appear, then their myriad progeny after
them,
Wondering, yearning, curious, with restless explorations,
With questioning, baffled, formless, feverish, with never-
happy hearts.

With that sad incessant refrain, Wherefore unstisfied
soul ? and Whither O mocking life?
Ah who shall soothe these feverish children ?
Who justify these restless explorations ? . . . . .
After the seas are all cross'd (as they seem already
cross'd),
After the great captains and engineers have accomplished
their work,
After the noble inventors, after the scientists, the chemist,
the geologist, ethnologist,
Finally shall come the poet worthy that name,
The true son of God shall come singing his songs.
Then not your deeds only O voyagers, O scientists and
inventors, shall be justified,
All these hearts as of fretted children shall be sooth'd,
All affection shall be fully responded to, the secret shall
be told,
All these separations and gaps shall be taken up and
book'd and link'd together . . . . . .
Passage to India !

Lo, soul, seest thou not God's purpose from the first ?
The earth to be spann'd connected by network,
The people to become brothers and sisters,
The races, neighbours, to marry and be given in marriage,
The oceans to be cross'd, the distant brought near,
The lands to be welded together.

One could quote indefinitely from Whitman moving passages on the subject of world union, cultural and religious. He stretched the powers of language to express the advent of the Great Society. "Omnes, omnes !" he cried and build his great poems around key-words like "rapport", "ensemble", "en-masse", "omnific", "omnigenous"; he spoke of the "knit of identity", dreamt of "unitary" societies and countries "forever entreatied"—"Inextricable lands! the clutch'd together"—

> Such join'd unended links, each hook'd to the next,
> Each answering all, each sharing the earth with all.

His poems simply burst with lines and phrases which might be inscribed in gold over the entrances to the General Assembly building of the United Nations : "I see . . . . the solidarity of races", -Are all nations communing? is there going to be but one heart to the globe? is humanity forming en-masse?"—"The earth, restive, confronts a new era". It is, so far, the measure of mankind's failure to meet the Vedantic challenge, Indian and American, that they have not been so inscribed.

Contemporary with the great Transcendentalists in America lived other fine writers such as Pope, Hawthorne, and Herman Melville who were often called inquisitors of this American Vedantism that I have been describing, and are represented as seeking to mock it out of court. On the other hand, it is quite possible to look on all these writers as born Vedantists who were stung into rage by men's widespread incapacity to rescue their true Self from the tangle of convention and miseducation that Emerson had decried. Many of Poe's stories, such as "The Black Cat" and "The Cask of Amontillado", are sheer tremors of horror caused by ignorant creatures' violation in others or even in animals, of the deep common life that operates by love and love only. At the end of his days Poe wrote a remarkable essay called "Eureka", in which are found passages like the following that rival Emerson attempts to express the mystery and nature of the All-One :

> All these creatures — all—those which you term animate as well as those to whom you deny life for no better reason than that you do not behold it in operation—all these creatures . . . . . are . . . . more or less conscious Intelligences; conscious, first, of a proper identity; conscious, secondly and by faint indeterminate glimpses, of an identity with the Divine Being of whom we speak—of an identity with God. Of the two classes of consciousness

> ness, fancy that the former will grow weaker, the latter stronger, during the long succession of ages which must elapse before these myriads of individual Intelligences become blended—when the bright stars become blended—into One. Think that the sense of individual identity will be gradually merged in the general consciousness—that Man, for example, ceasing imperceptibly to feel himself Man, will at length attain that awfully triumphant epoch when he shall recognise his existence as that of the Divine Ultimate. In the meantime bear in mind that even now all is Life—Life within life—the less within the greater, and all within the Spirit Divine.

Somewhat like Poe, Hawthorne seems to have thought of the common life in terms of which all creatures and all parts of the universe itself are organically interdependent as a form of chemical affinity or electromagnetic attraction. More often than not, the characters of his stories and novels learn about this interdependence and often too late, by breaking the electric circuit that binds each to all. Hawthorne never names the all-pervasive life the "Oversoul", but he makes dramatic use of the concept on many occasions, as when Clifford Pyncheon in The House of the Seven Gables, long shut off from his kind in prison, attempts to throw himself—from a high balcony—into the collective life of a great parade. Seen from a distance, we are told, a mighty procession :

> melts all the petty personalities of which it is made up into one broad mass of existence—one great life—one collected body of mankind, with a vast, homogeneous spirit animating if . . . . . if an impressionable person, standing alone over the brink of one of these procession, should behold it not in its atoms but in its aggregate—as a mighty river of life massive in its tide and black with mystery and, out of its depths, calling to the kindred depth within him—then the contiguity would add to the effect. It might so fascinate him that he would hardly be restrained from plunging into the surging streams of human sympathies.

So it proved with Clifford.

Melville, like both Hawthorne and Poe, is fascinated by the tragedies of men who try to isolate themselves from their fellow creatures. True, he found something more than repressed Brahman and fellow-feeling in what we now call the *unconscious mind*. If the common mind of all men—this Melville never rejects—be compared to an ocean, it will contain, he suggests, monstrous sharks and perhaps a great white whale which seems, at times at least, to be incarnate evil, but this evil, we may deduce from Moby Dick's whiteness, is chiefly the absence of good. It is nothing, but, of course, if we speak of the creative love by which man lives, nothing is more terrible than nothing. For this reason the white nothingness of evil has driven man to all his great creations in art and government —attempts to fill the white black-board with meaning and beauty. Describing the Pacific, the theatre of Moby Dick's operations, Melville elevates it into a marvellous symbol of Brahman.

> There is one knows not what sweet mystery about this sea, whose gentle awful stirrings seem to speak of some hidden soul beneath . . . . . for her millions of mixed shades and shadows, drowned dreams, somnambulisms, reveries—all that we call lives and souls—lie dreaming, still . . . .
>
> To any meditative Magian rover this serene Pacific, once beheld, must ever after be the sea of his adoption. It rolls the midmost waters of the world, the Indian Ocean and the Atlantic being but its arms. The same waves wash the moles of new-built California towns . . . . . and leave the faded but still gorgeous skirts of Asiatic lands, older than Abraham; while all between float milky-ways of coral isles and low-lying, endless unknown archipelagoes and impenetrable Japans. Thus this mysterious, divine Pacific Zones the world's whole bulk about; makes all coasts one bay to it; seems the tide-beating heart of earth.

> Lifted by those eternal swells, you needs must own the seductive god, bowing your head to Pan.

But few thoughts of Pan stirred Ahab's brain. . . . His impercipinence was the source of Ahab's madness and the tragedy of the Pequod.

Emerson's Oversoul was called by the poet Whittier "the Overheart", that is to say, a single heart-love spread through the manifold creation, and there was no New England poet or Boston Brahmin but was touched by, if not expert in, Vedantic lore. Oliver Wendell Holmes's so-called psychiatric novels were concerned in the 50's and 60's of the nineteenth century with deep disturbances in what the modern psychologist Carl Jung calls "the coilective unconscious", as love fights for existence in a world of people drearily and puritanically ignorant of the god within, but I need not stress the existence of Brahmanical thought among Brahmins like Holmes. It will be more useful to quote a few passages from modern American novelists to show the extent to which the idea of Brahman continues to animate American literature, even in the most unexpected places. Take, for instance, John Steinbeck's Grapes of Wrath. Tom Joad, who has just murdered a man is speaking :

> "Hm-m", he said. "Lookie, Ma. I been all day an, night hidin' alone, Guess who I been thin' about ? Casy! He talked a lot. Used ta bother me. But now I been thinkin' what he said, an' I can remember—all of it. Says one time he went out in the wilderness to find his own soul, an' he foun' he didn' have no soul that was his 'n' Says he foun' he jus' got a little piece of a great big soul. Says a wilderness ain't no good, 'cause his little piece of a soul wasn't no good' less it was with the rest, an' was whole. Funny how I remember. Didn' think I was even listenen'. But I know now a fella ain't no good alone".

Or take a popular novel like Carson McCullers' Member of the Wedding, which was made into an even more popular play. Here the whole problem of a girl's adolescent unease is treated in terms that can only be called cosmic, transcendental, advaitic. The novel tells how Frankie, a tiny, inadequate, fearful, "unoined" person, a mere dizzily unattached "I-person", *slowly matured into a "We-person", anxious to do*nate her blood so that it would flow in veins of men all over the globe—into a young woman who looked forward, finally. with Emersonian confidence to a time when "we will just walk up to people and know them right away . . . . . . We will have thousands of friends. . . . . . .we will belong to so many clubs that we can't even keep track of them *all*. We *will* be members of the whole world!" This passage reminds us of a similar one in Our Town, a play by Thornton wilder that is now acted by both professional and amateur groups all over America every year, in which a school boy talks to a school-girl, as they sit at a soda fountain, about the necessity, if we wish to be spiritually correct, of addressing mail not merely to Our Town, but to Our Town, in such-and-such a state, in the United States, in the northern half of the Western Hemisphere, in the world, in the Universe. . .

Or take Walter Van Tilburg Clark's Ox-Bow Incident, another American novel that enjoys wide popularity both as a book and motion picture. Just as Mrs. McCullers sees maturation in terms of the growth of planetary sympathies, Clark sees the mistaken lynching of a cattle man in the Old West not as a regrettable accident, not as a miscarriage of justice under the semi-barbarous conditions of a half-settled frontier, not as a *torticollis of the law of one nation, but as an Offence against* the jus gentium, the law of peoples, of mankind. The hanging of Martin is presented as a calamity for human beings throughout the world, for every man's life is necessarily and inescapably involved, whether he lives in the pasturelands of the half-tamed West or in the forest solitudes of India, with every other man's. Davies, the raisonneur of The Ox Bow Incident, speaks like a frontier Emerson, Whitman, Howthorne, and Holmes rolled into one when he says :

> "Law is more than the words that put it on the books; law is more than any decisions that may be made from it: law is more than the particular code of it stated at any

> one time or in any one place or nation; more than any man, lawyer or judge, sheriff, or jailer who may represent it. True law, the code of justice, the essence of our sensations of right and wrong, is the conscience of society. It has taken thousands of years to develop, and it is the greatest, the most distinguishing quality which has evolved with mankind. None of man's temples, none of his religions, none of his weapons, his tools, his arts, his sciences, nothing else he has grown to, is so great a thing as. . . . . . . his sense of justice. The true law is something in itself; it is the spirit of the moral nature of man; it is an existence apart, like God, and as worthy of worship as God. If we can touch God, at all, where do we touch him save in the conscience? And what is the conscience of any man save his little fragment of the conscience of all men in all time?"

Convictions like the above constitute, I would say, both the main subject and the decorative arabesques, the theme and the variations, of practically all significant American literature from Emerson to the present. This Vedantic Voice in American literature is possibly its genuinely characteristic and original voice. Only Indians can recognize how old this originality really is! Vedantism, East and West, is an answer to the great human need to find order, purpose, and homogeneity in the chaos of phenomena. Without some such simplification and unification of experience, the mind, overburdened with the problem of understanding, seems to sicken. Hygienically, and unerringly, then, the men and women who have made American literature have sought and found sanity in a quarter well cultivated in India for twenty-five hundred years—this fact argues, then, that the study of American literature might from a surprisingly congenial part of English studies, both graduate and undergraduate, in what used to be known in America as "the immortal land of the deathless" "Bhagavat-Geeta".

21

The Impact of American Criticism on Modern Indian Scholarship*

F.R. Leavis for a message in the anniversary of an English Seminar, in his characteristic way and in his scrawl of handwriting with its ups and downs and twirls, he wrote with the kind of forthrightness which he possesses, that we should confine ourselves to an "otherness" so far as English Studies in India are concerned. The message impinged on our minds and we thought seriously that there could be an "otherness" of critical approach which would emanate out of an Indian ethos or sensibility. English Literature is widely studied in different countries: In Italy, for example, Dr. Camillo Pelizzi who held the Chair of Italian in London University, for sometime, looked at the Englishman as perhaps an Englishman would never do for himself. In his book English Drama he wrote: 'The inner Englishman is Saxon in race and instincts, but he has taken his religion and many other civil institutions from Rome, his Bible from the Jew, his formulating organism from the gallicised Normans, his culture from Athens, Rome, Paris'. Pelizzi's whole perspective of drama was from the

---

* An address to the delegates of Indian and American Universities at the American Literature Seminar held at Banaras Hindu University in February, 1963.

point of view of the English character as observed by an European. He found the Englishman with his conservatism given to compromise: 'Compromise', he wrote, 'is the important thing. It will remain as long as England remains in history, and it solves all the problems of the English enigma; even that of the drama from Shakespeare to Shaw'. He found, as a whole, a great tradition and a few slants in creation of criticism.

What concerned Pelizzi was the problem of race in the evaluation of English Literature—a problem which may on rare occasions give a distorted view as in Othello's character, for example, even as he utters lines like 'I do confess the vices of my blood' or 'These Moors are changeable in their wills'. But ethos is fairly a good stabilizing factor in the character of a critic; it gives him a certain equilibrium and a healthy steadfastness to certain norms which he values.

There is such a thing as an Indian ethos which can be got from a study of the literature in Sanskrit and the regional languages. The critical works in these languages are also fairly effective guides. By race and character the Indian is given to metaphysics and philosophy and he tries to express them in a language removed from common life. That is why Alankara or figures of speech mattered so much in the works of theorists of criticism like Bharata, Anandavardhana, Abhinavagupta, Mammata, Visvanatha, or Jagannatha of Banaras. More than the denotation of words or their contextual meaning, the suggestive meaning or 'Dhwani' was largely observed in its rich array. There was no serious attempt at a literary evaluation or practical criticism of the Western type even for such a great dramatist as Kalidasa.

In the British period when English was first introduced in Macaulay's plan of education, the Indians went into ruptures as they read the English Romantics—Tagore's poetry is influenced by that trend. Sonorousness and euphony gave suggestive meaning in their fullness and Burke's addressess and Carlyle's majestic flows of diction in the French Revolution led to an English style of musical nuances and fortissimo found in the English writings of Srinivas Sastri.

The students of literature read Shakespeare with an

emotional gusto. The late Professor P.C. Ghosh of Calcutta University attracted students from other Universities and I still remember his weeping as he read Desdemona's murder. Many of us lost our manhood and wept with him.

When it came to research in English, philosophy was the first attraction. Platonism in Spenser was an early thesis and Cazamian wrote a laudatory foreword for both Legouis and *Cazemian find literature good metaphysics in their History* of English Literature. A young scholar went to England and wrote a thesis *on Shakespeare and Kalidasa,* and was awarded the doctorate degree from Durham University. The thesis was a struggle between sensibility and rhetoric. Saintsbury's A History of Criticism became a kind of Poetics and several Indian scholars went the Saintsbury way—the sensitive soul's journey through masterpieces. Impressionistic criticism, discursive and rambling at times, with more of feeling and emotion than cerebration, was the kind of early response to English literature and poetry especially. A few who wanted to get out of the muddle went to Oxford and other English Universities and sought out quaint and rare authors: one wrote a whole thesis on only two plays by Robert Wilson, a sixteenth century dramatist and another on Lyttleton. A voyage across the seas gave dignity to research and one went to London University for a thesis on Anglo-Indian Poetry the materials of which were available in India. Another who did not know Bengali went to Montpellier (France) and got his doctorate *degree on Tagore through English translations,* at the time when the poet was alive and half-way through his creative writings and criticism. There was a teacher who held his emotions with suspect and got a doctorate degree from Oxford *University on Middle English Grammar. There is till one* alive of that generation whose magnum opus is Cynewulf which has passed out of the syllabus of several Indian Universities.

Since the attainment of independence there has been a sharp change in Indian scholarship and methodology in criticism. The impressionistic criticism which had its own aesthetics in the cult of beauty formulated by Walter Peter or concepts based on organic wholes as in Bradley's Shakespearean Criticism gave way to books like Armstrong's Shakespeare's Imagination which is based on psycho-analysis. Language or linguistic knowledge received a new emphasis from a book like Richards and Ogden The Meaning of Meaning or A.P. Rossitter: Angel with Horns. F.R. Leavis and the Cambridge school in England with 'close and relevant thinking' advocated in The Common Pursuit and numbers of the Scrutiny, led Indian students of literature to literary evaluation of that type. T.S. Eliot too made his impact on Indian scholarship with his Selected Essays and other writings. As a matter of fact the only antithesis in critical methods well understood by Indian students is that between F.R. Leavis and T.S. Eliot.

The Indo-American cultural contacts virtually began as a post-Independence phenomenon after 1947. The Ford Foundation and the U.S.I.S. centres in India contributed books and journals to Indian Universities. It was at this stagè that Indian scholarship received a new and organised creative and critical stimulus It is gratifying for the Indian scholar to find the large number of original documents and manuscripts which are not in the British Museum but in American possession. Recently for example, an unpublished letter of Hazlitt appeared in the June, 1962, number of the PMLA. The letter dated 5th November, 1809, is preserved at the Massachusetts Historical society. It throws light on Hazlitt, his relations, friends including the Lambs, and his literary activities at Winterslow.

American research on English themes is read with avidity and discrimination by Indian students and teachers. Egon Stephen Merton's book, to take a stray example, Science and Imagination published by Columbia University in 1949, assessed Sir Thomas Browne, not in the movement of thought of Spinoza or Descartes or in the unified sensibility of the metaphysicals as is done in the later British book of Basil Willey: The Seventeenth Century Background (1957), but in the essence of Browne's circle of being where the circumference is science and the centre, his imagination. Merton in effect expounded the causes of those 'enchanting forms' which Edmund Gosse mentioned ad passim.

To my mind the greatest impact of American criticism is in the field of applied rather than theoretical research. The Indian scholar works under severe limitations and handicaps: shortage of books and journals, lack of microfilms or photostats of manuscripts and documents, and a nostalgia for pleasing English scholarship of the type found in Sir Walter Raleigh or Middleton Murry. What the research worker, particularly the young, desire is new techniques to get new results. Kenneth Burke, the American Aristotle, has in some essentials, an influence on Indian research. His judgment values and the processes which lead to them give the student of literature the necessary discipline, sharpness of perception and objectivity, essential in criticism. In his book Counter-Statement there is the chapter 'Lexicon Rhetoricae' in which he discusses the methods of analysis. A poem or a literary work has 'syllogistic progression' or a logical seuence of ideas and from which are inevitable, Browning's Prospice, for example, moves and ends as expected: 'Fear death?—want death. Different from 'syllogistic Progression' is what Kenneth Burke calls 'qualitative progression' or a movement in which the end is just the opposite of what a reader anticipates. There is an example of this in a passage in Arnold's Thyrsis. Arnold, a poet of opposites, as the American critic, Lional Trilling, estimates him, had a romantic sensibility which was largely suppressed because of his scepticism. In a mood of romantic exultation he wrote:

'So have I heard the cuckoo's parting cry,
From the Wet field, through the vet garden-trees,
Come with the Volleying rain and tossing breeze'—

and just as one is lifted in this mood looking for a climax of expression, the mood just folds up :

'The bloom is gone, and with the bollm go I'.

Cleanth Brooks is an American critic whose technique finds favour in India. In The Well Wrought Urn he writes of paradox as the essential of poetry. Paradox and the subtlety of it is an element for critical observation. Cleanth Brooks is one of a group, the New Critics like John Crowe Ransom, Allen Tata and Robert Penn Warren whose object can be discovered from Ransom's The New Criticism (1941). The technique of these critics is to study a work of literature by itself within its own autonomy unrelated to extraneous considerations like history, biography and even 'The Affective Fallacy' of response as discussed in Wimsatt's The Verbal Icon (1954). This method has its validity. John Wain exemplifies it in that stimulating book of critiques Interpretations. T.S. Eliot has a gibe at this book and calls this type of criticism 'the lemon-squeezer' type of criticism. But then, I ask, what else can you do with a lemon but to squeeze it ?

The Indian scholar has accepted largely but not wholly the technique of the New Critics : he cannot quite do so absolutely because of its partial doctrine of aesthetics and method. In a large measure the New Criticism helps practical criticism of a short poem. But for longer works one finds the technique of the Chicago school of critics useful. In the mid-thirties a group of scholar-critics led by R.S. Crane, poet and Professor Emeritus of English at the University of Chicago, considered the totality of a work of art rather than its parts, except in its relations to the whole, as the proper field for investigation. They found the Aristotelian method of considering plot or wholeness with 'maximum differentiation' without destruction of 'universals' as the just critical method. The critics of this school are called neo-Aristotelians although their purpose was to enlarge the resources of criticism, with Aristotle as a starting point but going beyond him in a continuity of his method applied to modern writing. In fact, they wrote as profoundly of Plato, Longiuns, Johnson and Coleridge as they did of Aristotle. Their main consideration is the theory of aesthetics as part of philosophy : they regard a poem or a work of art as an ordered and complete whole. This fullness in an approach is stimulating Indian research. There is an Indian research scholar under me working on Dylan Thomas. He is engaged in an exciting exparimenti. He has taken as his methodology the structure and texture technique of the New Critics together with the totality method of the Chicago critics especially Elder Olson. The results he has got so far are substantial and promising. Still, I feel, an Indian seholar's sensibility is towards empathy or the identification of the reader with the poem or the work of art : this helps him to enjoy literature, an act which few modern critics can do. Even objectively there is the consideration of the lyrical which is often lost in a grammar of criticism or a totality which includes knowledge. The Indian scholar therefore finds some kinship even with an anti-critic of the New Critics like Van Doren who will not inhibit himself with methods of criticism which arrest the lyrical flight in a poem or a work of literature.

There is another aspect of modern American criticism, namely, its use of non-literary knowledge and techniques for literary ends. Psychology, the social sciences and anthropology have been used with their growing knowledge to explain the thought patterns and the symbols in which the creative artist transmits his experience. In 1912 Jane Ellen Harrison of Newnham College, Cambridge, wrote Themis : A Study of the Social Origins of Greek Religion in which she analysed Greek drama from the stand-point of ritualistic forms or anthropology, a trend taken up by Maud Bodkin in Archetypal Patterns of Poetry. In *1919* Conrad Aiken, the poet, wrote Scepticisms in which he used psychology, particularly, Freudism, for a study of poetry. Five years later in 1924 in England, I.A. Richards published his *Principles of Literary* Criticism, a work in which he took the finding of psychology under impulese, desires and motives to explain experience and communication.

This type of criticism in which one uses knowledge for evaluation finds favour with the Indian scholar. He uses *psychology and this accounts for a number* of good dissertations and papers in Indian Universities on the Romantic poets and the stream of consciousness novel. The Indian slant however is *towards Orientalism* or a *study* of English and American literature in relation to Indian thought and philosophy or Indian Semantics or Rhetoric. The critical method employed is laborious, scholarly and perspicuous, much like what the American critic R.P. Blackmur does.

The Indian scholar does not dispense with historical criticism : that is still his business in a phase of his investigations. There is also the problem of epistemology or knowledge and reality or subject and object—a problem which preoccupies Melvilla's heroes who always ask can we really "know" anything ? Epistemology helps in a study of the writings of Sri Aurobindo which is a major field of research in India today. Obviously such subjects provoke the use of new methods of criticism or new co-ordinates as presented by the European critic Jacques Maritain or isolated American critics who regard literature or poetry as ontology.

American criticism is playing a major part in giving the Indian scholar a valid and good judgment technique. Added to this is what emerges from his own sensibility and ethos. These help him to evolve a critical method, mainly eclectic in character, which takes the best critical procedures of his own country and that of other lands.

22

Drama and the Mirror up to Nature

Ford Madox Ford in *The March of Literature* has given us the axiom that the quality of literature is 'the quality of humanity'. The appeal of literature is due to the communication between the writer and the reader on a plane where the secrets of the human heart and the story of human viccisitudes are revealed. With this *sine qua non* drama is the form of literature which best reveals human life.

Greek dramatists for a century or more and the Elizabethans from 1590-1640, an odd fifty years, presented life with all its passions and foibles and situations in which characters derived their slant and in turn begot situations. This interplay of character and situation was brought out by playwrights with an eye to verisimilitude or plausibility.

Shakespeare in *Hamlet*, III, 2, analysed drama when he wrote that its main purport is 'to hold as't' were the mirror up to nature'. Drama became a faithful representation of life true to 'human motives, character and speech'. This is the universality which Shakespeare presents and which is the truth, as Allardyce Nicoll writes, in fable or in the borrowed stories of Shakespeare.

A survey of Shakespeare's plays presents the universality of humanity even in the particular condition of the characters or the acuteness of the situations in which they are found. Hamlet, for example, deals with human inadequacy. Hamlet is burdened with the religious responsibility, according to Elizabethan spiritualism, the thesis of Dover Wilson in *What Happens in Hamlet*, to murder his uncle but he succumbs under the weight of his task and even from the very first soliloquy utters about this human weakness in the lines :

> 'O cursed spite,
> That ever I was born to set it right! ' (Act I, Sc. V)

Macbeth by secret self-division becomes a psychopath as F.L. Lucas says in *Literature and Psychology*. His qualms of conscience are true to life as he states : 'if the assassination

> Could trammel up the consequence' (Act I, Sc. VII)

Lady Macbeth too shows the weakness of womanhood in the sleep-walking scene. In the Comedies too women act true to life with their several variants of character as to Rosalind, Beatrice and Viola.

Shakespeare in the amplitude of his vision of life gave to himself the necessary creative freedom for good and great art. In *As You Like It* he wrote with this end in view :

> 'I must have liberty
> Withal, as large a character as the wind,
> To blow on whom I please'. (Act 2, Scene 7)

Sidney Lee commenting on the sweeping comprehensiveness of Shakespeare's plays writes that good and bad, rich or poor, old and young, as a matter of fact, every type of individual lent him their secrets and his genius enabled him to give them life in his pages. The presentation of human life was Shakespeare's main point; he did not aim at an ethical view of life as did Webster in *The White Devil* or *The Duchess of Malfi*, the concluding lines of which plays indicate the didactic purpose of the plays. Grierson in *Cross Currents in Seventeenth Century Literature* draws out this distinction between the human and the ethical approach of Shakespeare and Webster respectively.

It has always been a mistaken method to approach Shakespeare's plays as if they are nothing beyond 'a mirror held up to nature'. In the *Hamlet* context from where the phrase is taken there are other important aspects of drama which Shakespeare enunciates together with the idea of holding the mirror up to nature'. *Hamlet* says that drama also should embody' 'the very age and body of the time his form and pressure', in other words, that drama should be contemporaneous. Shakespeare actually does that in his plays. For example, the historical plays, *Richard II, Henry IV* Parts I and II, *Henry V*, deal with the past but in the light of contemporary theme, such as, the Tudor theory of the Divine Right of Kings, the unity of England and England's supremacy abroad. In all good plays the contemporaneous is engrafted on the theme from whichever age it is taken, such as, the description of the very English mob in *Julius Caesar* or the London of the times in Ben Jonson's *Bartholomew Fair.*

Shakespeare was a man of the theatre and he wrote his plays as J. Isaacs states, in the actuality of the theatre. He criticizes players and acting in *Hamlet.* In *Antony and Cleopatra* he realizes the limitations of the stage in the presentation of human life, as Cleopatra says in Act V scene 2 :

> 'the quick comedians
> Extemporally will stage us',

where Antony will appear as a drunk and Cleopatra portrayed by 'some squeaking Cleopatra boy' referring to the boy-actor who will play the part of the queen of Egypt. Shakespeare's analysis of the drama, therefore, is first, that it shuld be a reflection of life or 'hold the mirror up to nature'; second, that it should contain contemporaneous matter; and third, that it should be properly staged and acted.

Elizabethan drama is generally based itself on the presentation of human life from *The Arden of Feversham* to Shakespeare's *Coriolanus* (excluding the Romances). The idea of holding the mirror up to nature was diversely viewed through the ages. Dr. Johnson, supporting Neander in Dryden's *Essay on Dramatic Poety* who pointed out that tragi-comedy is something which the ancients and the moderns did not know, writes that 'the stage pretends only to be the mirror of life'. All drama, as E.E. Stoll writes, deals with an illusion. The successful dramatist makes the audience surrender to that illusion. Eugene O'Neill commenting on Strindberg writes that 'Old Naturalism is holding the family kodak up to ill nature'. O'Neill believes that realism or naturalism is not enough but that there should be a super-naturalism which shows the mystery of life as he wrote in *The Great God Brown* : 'Mystery--the mystery any one man or woman can feel but not understand . . . . . I want to realize in the theatre'.

Naturalism in drama got a new fillip in the Modern Theatre. Dramatists gave excerpts from life without any gloss. Robertson, the originator of realistic production on the stage, heralded the period with his plays *Society* and *Caste*. H.A. Jones in the preface to his play *Saints and Sinners*, a satire on ordinary men and women, put as his goal 'not spectacular illusion but the art of representing English life'. Other plays with a realistic trend are pinero's *The Second Mrs. Tranqueray* and Granvilla Baker's *The Voysey Inheritance*.

Ibsen, the Norwegian dramatist, did for drama what Baudelaire did for Eliot's poetry. Ibsen focussed the attention of the dramatist to contemporary problems. He took a clinical attitude to life. He himself wrote that his concern was not 'glaciers and pine forests but what is going on in the silent hearts of the people'. He diagnosed life and exposed the humbug and hypocrisy of respectable society in plays like *A Doll's House*. There he shows the absurdity and the falsity of prudery and Nora's revolt is a flouting of Victorian respectability.

Ibsen intensified and magnified the problems of life and in this he actually revolutionised the English and the European theatre. Ideas were more important than ideals and Ibsen's influence on dramatists was phenomenal. His influence has been acknowledged by Archer, Pinero, Jones and Shaw. Shaw wrote a paper on him in admiration, The Quintessence of Ibsenism, even as he wrote one on Wagner in his stimulating work Wagnerism.

J.T. Grein, a Dutchman, in 1889 made the first attempt to stage Ibsen in the English Theatre. Shaw followed Ibsenite plays and devoted his whole career to diagnose life's problems as they presented themselves in his own age. Like Ibsen he attacked conventions of religion and society and 'turned the footlights to illuminate personal and private problems'. Shaw laughed out of the Theatre the romantic falsities and pruderies of life. In Widowers' Houses he dealt with the problem of *landlordism*. The characters are shown as *hypocrites and* humbugs. Trench is an ignorant sentimentalist; Blanche Sartorius is a designing minx. In Mrs. Warren's Profession he deals with the problems of prostitution. In Arms and the Man he makes a 'general onslaught on idealism' as he *writes in the* Preface and exposes this through the ridiculousness of Raina with her heroworship and the bluntness of the chocolate soldier, Bluntschli, who says, 'I'm a professional soldier, I fight when I have to, and am very *glad to get out of* it when I haven't to'. In this play he debunks the romantic pretences of war. Candida is written in the spirit of the New Women's Movement or as Marchbanks says, 'She means that she belongs to herself'. *Her typical Shavian superiority is* seen in the words 'I give myself to the weaker of the two'.

Besides problem plays, Shaw writes historical plays, such as, Caesar and Cleopatra, St. Joan. These plays are anachronistic in spirit. Caesar and Cleopatra as presented by Shaw are ironically and satirically conceived. Shaw, the inveterate jester, makes Cleopatra on Caesar's knee, pat his bald pate and suggest as hair restorer. Shaw also writes plays with ideas such as Mand and Superman and *Back to Methuselah*. He tries to popularise current scientific theories. He deals with Life Force which according to him is a combination of biological evolution and eugenics.

All these plays of Shaw reveal a *realistic approach to current problems*. Plays like the Apple Cart, Too True to be good, On the Rocks, Geneva are mostly topical commentaries upon the European nightmare. In Plays Pleasant and Unpleasant Shaw dispels the conventions and *ostentations of English society*. His brilliant wit and gift for reparatee make his characters excellent talkers. Shaw makes a fool of every character in some way or other.

Among other innovators of the *naturalistic play is John Galsorthy*. *In his* essay Some Platitudes concerning Drama (in The Inn of Tranquility) he writes of 'Naturalistic technique' and compares Naturalistic art to 'a steady lamp, help up from time to time, in whose light things will be seen for a space clearly and in due proporation, freed from the mists of pre-justice and partisanship'. He thus gives us transcripts from life or social phenomena. In Strife he deals with industrial conflict—the 'No Compromise' of John Antony and the 'No surrender' of David Roberts, the men's leader. The deadlock is removed by the death of Robert's wife. In The Silver Box and Justice he deals with the problems of the law. He is against the crushing of the individual by society. Justice is a commentary on the prison administration of the period. The Judge in condemning Falder says, 'The Law is what it is—'and thereby gives his sanction to its immutability and implacability. The play was conceived to show the disproportion between the seriousness of an offence and the weight of punishment which society might lay upon the offender through the agency of blind Justice. Although Galsworthy claims in The Inn of Tranquility to follow impersonality in drama he allows his sentiment to give colour to the play. This is especially seen in Strife where the death of Mrs. Robert ends the turmoil between labour and capital, the strain of humanitarianism arising out of the death, having nothing to do with the real problem of Strife.

Antithetical to Galsworthy's methods of drama in the naturalistic play are those employed by Harley Granville Barker. Whereas Galsworthy deals with the individual in 'society', Barker deals with the individual and the intimidation of 'convention'. In The Voysey Inheritance he deals with the problem of absolute honesty. Voysey, a solicitor, dies leaving £ 100,000 which he gathers by perpetrating several frauds on his clients. He confesses to his son, Edward, just before his death of his fraudulent methods. Edward accepts the inheritance, but later asks the family to surrender their legacies. The whole play is a struggle between rectitude and self-interest.

Shaw, Galsworthy and Granville Barker, like Jones, Robertson, and Pinero, revived naturalistic drama as a reproduction of contemporary life. They did not, like Shakespeare and the Elizabethan dramatists, deal with humanity as such; they are concerned with the new naturalism *which deals with current problems of modern life* as initiated by Ibsen and given various turns by English dramatists.

There are a few dramatists in modern times who while dealing with actual life, work out their basic philosophy of life through the medium of realism. Eugene O'Neill is one such dramatist. In Strange Interlude he utters his main theme in the words of Nina Leeds : 'Our lives are merely strange, dark interludes in the electrical display of God the Father'. T.S. Eliot too imposes his first principles by conscious art in his plays. Murder in the Cathedral is part and parcel of Christian worship. *The Family Reunion is a drama of sin* and expiation. Harry is guilty of evil desire as his father and Agatha before him. In this play Eliot too uses the contemporary *situation*. He links the ritual of primitive fear with the twentieth century drawing room and deals with the complex of attitudes and the burden guilt. In The Cocktail Party he deals with the problem of salvation in the character of Celia as she is murdered by an ant hill.

Naturalism, although it flourished considerably from the '90s to the '30s met with a conscious revolt by a group of formidable artists, such as, *Clifford Bax, Ashley Dukes* and Gordon Craig, the son of Ellen Terry. They revived poetic plays and among the great poet-playwrights are Lord Dunsany, *Clifford Bax, T.S. Eliot, John Drinkwater* and Christopher Fry. Fry is by far the most colourful and most poetic dramatist to-day. He has written plays like The Lady's Not for Burning, Venus Observed, A Sleep of Prisoners, in which he brings out the richness of English diction. He takes realistic problems like the polygamist's predicament in Venus Observed and works them out into symbols. A Sleep of Prisoners is almost a Passion Play with its great poetry and vision before which its initial realism of captured prisoners disappears. The poetic play appears to have come to stay in the English theatre. But whether the realistic play has ended, *is disputable, for* the reality of drama, like the reality of fiction, is actual life, in theme and speech.

23

Criticism of Moments

The object of this paper is to establish a tenable and valid norm of criticism or, what I may term, the criticism of moments. There is the normal and continuous way of judgment-values through tradition and individual talent or through a judicious use of both interpretative and historical criticism. In the course of a major study of an author or the working out of a literary problem, one comes by illuminating minor points, rather insufficient in quantity to establish a characteristic or trend or even to give a new alignment to the subject. These ad passim discoveries remain unused in Notebooks or confined to the memory and, for all their worth, are no better than waste products. Criticism of moments is a thrifty form of criticism and has for purpose the utilization of these passing findings. They can be worked out into notes or papers. Criticism of moments, although the term is analogous to Virginia Woolf's novels of moments, does not follow any depth psychology or stream of consciousness technique ; on the contrary, it can achieve the high level of objectivity and impersonality.

In Memoriam is a well-known poem and it is through it that I desire to exemplify the nature and effects of criticism of moments. The major assessments in Tennyson have been done, by and parge, unless there is a new letter or diary of

Tennyson or that of his friends, acquaintances or relations, which could shed new light on the poet. He is a representative poet of his age (Hugh Walkar); he is primarily an artist (Henry Jones); he is commonplace in his thoughts and hence A.C. Bradley's 'Reaction against Tennyson'. He had desired to write a long poem (Abercrombie); he possessed the vitality of doubt rather than faith (Eliot). Such and similar are the authoritative views on the poet.

Studying In Memoriam even along these broad and correct perspectives, a modern student of literature is moved to literary fervour or mixed moods of reception which he senses may be just straws in the wind or, on a later reconsideration of the poem, lead to some rich haystack of summer time. Helen Gardner in The Business of Criticism (1959) writes of this later process in criticism :

> 'The enlarging and continual reforming of one's conception of a work by bringing fresh knowledge and fresh experience of life and literature to it, this process of continual submission and resubmission to the work is highly delightful and perpetually renews the original sense of delight from which the critic began.'[1]

Tennyson's imagery is largely romantic, after the legacy received by the Victorians from their elders in an earlier age. Tennyson writes of 'silver sleep' (XI), 'silver flame' (LXVII) clinging to the word 'silver' as Keats had done in over-abundance in his poetry (Wilson Knight : The Starlit Dome). He has other Keatsian texture in his poetry e g. 'purple-frosty bank' (CVII) *recalling* 'purple-stained mouth' (Ode to a Nightingale). He writes of 'dewy-tassell'd wood' (LXXXVI), a Keatsian compound. He has a happy recalling of Wordsworth's Tintern Abbey in his 'babbling Wye' (XIX), an abbreviation after the generic picture style which was Tennyson's manner as it was of the Victorians like William Morris, *for example, with his description of the sea in single adjectives* in The Earthly Paradise.

Tennyson has a turn at Wordsworth's ante-natal theory or the doctrine of anamnesis when he writes of the child : 'he forgets the days before' (XLIV). There are singular Shelleylean lines in Tennyson of the intense inane e.g. 'In shadowy thoroughfares of thought' or 'Cloud-Towers by ghostly masons Wrought' (LXX).

To such a nineteenth century sensibility, comes in passing, the experiences of modern poets. One could never fancy that Tennyson could write or anticipate Hilda Doolittle, for example, as he does in this instance :

> 'Where all the starry heavens of space
> Are sharpen'd to a needle's end' (LXXVI).

The needle image is analogous to Hilda Doolittle's Imagist poem, Oread, with its concretization of sea waves to pine needles :

> 'Whirl up sea,
> Whirl your pointed pines.
> Splash your great pines
> On our rocks.'

F.W. Bateson in English Poetry : A Critical Introduction (1950) writes of romantic schizophrenia in Tennyson.[2] The poet was divided in his allegiance between the poetic ideal of beauty of the Victorians and his inner leanings for socialism. W.H. Auden observes the same absence of interest in social changes when he compares Tennyson with Baudaleire and finds in the two poets an absence of social consciousness :

> 'The same difference shows itself in their respective attitudes to society and personal relations. Both were professedly lonely men who viewed the loud gregarious extrovert with fear and distaste.'[3]

Notwithstanding all this, the 'social ego' in Tennyson is perceived in a few distinct passages in In Memoriam. In paragraph CVI the bells of the New Year ring out 'the feud of rich and poor' and as he specifically refers to his age :

> 'Ring out the want, the care, the sin,
> The faithless coldness of the times.'

This Section, for the greater part, is Tennyson's 'programme poem' akin to Stephen Spender's more specific 'programme poem', 'Not palaces, an era's crown' :

> 'No man
> Shall hunger : Man shall spend equally.
> Our goal which we compel : Man shall be man.'

Like Spender, Tennyson's lyricism in paragraph CVI had a social content; but, unlike Spender, to be fair in observation, Tenny son had not any particular social ideology as Spender was constrained to express in the Preface to The Still Centre : 'I have decidedly supported one side the Republican…'. Tennyson is a typical Benthamite in his liberalism as he vouchsafes utilitarianism in the last line of the sixth stanza of the same paragraph under reference : 'Ring in the common love of good'. In the later paragraph, CXXVII, he writes with passion, social awareness, and a historical sense of the French Revolution :

> 'Well roars the storm to those that hear
> A deeper voice acrose the storm,
> Proclaiming social truth shall spread,
> And justice, ev'n tho' thrice again
> The red fool-fury of the Seine
> Should pile her bar icades with dead.'

Tennyson in this social trend can be in a study of literary genetice, considered as a precursor of the poets of the 1930s—although, it must be said, the trend is elementary and remained undeveloped as he pursued Victorian tradition with its 'nostalgia for those Happy Isles'. Tennyson was conditioned by his age : still it is exhilarating to find incipient potentialities in him of new forces which developed so powerfully in the early Spender-Auden-Mayokovsky group.

The Victorian age was poor in producing the poet-critic type. Except Coventry Patmore's Prefatory Study on English Matrical Law (1879), there appears to be no organized study of the problems of poetry by a poet. The twentieth century is recondite with critical theories expounded by poets like A.E. Housman, Edith Sitwell, T.E. Hulme, Herbert Read, Cecil Day Lewis, Ezra Pound and T.S. Eliot. Although Tennyson had no tract on the theory of poetry, the poet in In Memoriam is preoccupied with the problem of communication. He feels the inadequacy of language to express his experience :

> 'For words, like Nature, half-reveal
> And half-conceal the Soul within' (V).

In later Verses he writes of his 'poor flower of Poesy' (VIII) and the spontaneity of his lyricism :

> 'I do but sing because I must,
> And pipe but as the linnets sing' (XXI).

He reverts again to the problem of words :

> 'My words are only words, and moved
> Upon the topmost froth of thougth' (LII).

He emerges from all this vagueness to surer ground but all that in a momentary percipience, as he writes of 'fitting aptest words to thing' (LXXV). This virtually tantamounts to an emphasis of the precision of language which according to Eliot along with economy of words, is the chief constituent of poetry achieved by Dryden and missed by Shalley and the Romantics.[4] In the text of the Four Quartets, Eliot like Tennyson, creatively considers his own assessment of the language of poetry :

> 'Where every world is at home
> Taking its place to suggest the others
> The common word exact without vulgarity,
> The formal word precise but not pedantic'
> (Little Gidding)

But Tennyson could not gather into focus of detail, like Eliot, the flash he had of 'fitting aptest words to things'. Like great artists, Tennyson was conscious of the poetic process in the course of his composition. His emphasis, however, on the tonal or aural effects in poetry affected, to a measure, his understanding of language and its denotative use in poetry. The problem of communication was touched upon by Tennyson but in a timid way, much like what he did in the realm of thought.[5]

There are other germinal ideas in Tennyson leading to Eliot as the Wisdom-Knowledge gradation in CXIV : 'She (Knowledge) is the second, not the first (Wisdom) recalling Eliot's famous lines beginning 'Where is the wisdom we have lost in knowledge'.

Tennyson, writes John Murray Moore, is 'a kind of ornithologist'.[6] He has several passages on birds, their beauty and their flight, such as,

> 'Wild bird, whose warble, liquid sweet,
> Rings Eden thro' the budded quicks' (LXXXVIII)

or 'The lark hath left the lea' (LXVIII) or 'The lark becomes a sightless song' (CXV), or 'the mounted thrust' (XCI) or the kingfisher, 'the sea-blue bird of March' (XCI). His awareness of the beauty of birds anticipates Robert Bridges who wrote several poems on birds and within whose artistic experience :

> 'Birds are of all animals the nearest to men for that they take delight in both music and dance, and gracefully schooling leisure to enliven life Wer the earlier artists'.

The Testamant of Beauty,
Book I, LL, 106-109.

All these points of contact between Tennyson and the moderns like Hilda Doolittle, Stephen Spender, T.S. Eliot and Robert Bridges, occur in passing while reading or re-reading Tennyson. In writing of them, one gets a small and useful collection or an exercise in criticism of moments. Through memorabilia an effective understanding of poetry is achieved both in an historical and interpretative way. Tennyson's Victorian sensibility, for example, stands out boldly against the antithesis of the referentials of modern poetry. Even if this is partially achieved, the converse too has happened : the pinpointing of certain aspects of modern poetry observed anew against the background of the *Victorian age or a Victorian* poet. This is precisely what R.P. Blackmur does when he applies Tennyson's view that he knew the quantity of every word except that he knew the quantity of every word except that in the word 'scissors' with vowels sandwiched between double consonants, to establish the relation of metre and rhythm and the musical phrase in modern poets like Yeats, Pound and Eliot.[7]

Moments in criticism are not *identical to impressionistic* criticism based on subjectivism like Pater's Appreciations or that naive book on Eliot's poetry by children and persons of different age groups or callings, Neville Braybrooke's T.S. Eliot : A Symposium for his Seventieth Birthday (1958).[8] Critical intelligence plays its part even in criticism of moments. The only caution is, it will do well to heed, is not to pervert the estimate of the poet by straitjacketing it within the framework of one's *selected or isolated findings. This type of* approach has marred William Archer's The Old Drama and the New where appraisals of the Elizabethans, like Webster, are made from the stand-point of Ibsenite dramaturgy.

There are byways in literature like publications never meant to be so such as, the Diary of Semuel Pepye, the Diary of Richard Symonds or the Paston letters or publications of the Camden Society. There is gold to find even in all these nuggets. *Criticism of moments is identical in value. It makes* study engaging and rewarding. It gives literary delight and saves criticism from its Dryasdust humdrum which 'professionalism' and excessive specialization bring in their trail.

REFERENCES

1. The Business of Criticism by Helen Gardner, (1959), p. 15.
2. English Poetry by F.W. Bateson, (1950), pp. 223-33.

3. Tennyson: An Introduction and a Selection by W.H. Auden (1946), Introd., p. XIX.
4. Selected Essays by T.S. Eliot (1932), 'John Dryden'.
5. Tennyson by Henry Jones (1909). Of the poet's thought, Jones wrote: 'He touched great themes in a timid way', p. 8.
6. Three Aspects of the late Alfred, Lord Tennyson by John Murray Moore (1901), p. 26.
7. Language as Gesture by R.P. Blackmur (1954), Essay: Lord Tennyson's Scissors, 1912-1950, pp. 422-40.
8. T.S. Eliot : A Symposium for his Seventieth Birthday by Neville Braybrooke, (1958). Rose Macaulay's study on 'The Wasteland' is a poor essay at that, pp. 29-33.

24

W.B. Yeats : A Study in Partial and Total Experience

Even the great W.B. Yeats has suffered from a fallacy of perspectives. R.P. Blackmur in Language as Gesture writes that Yeate is 'not one of the greatest poets', that 'he could not create, except in fragments the actuality of his age'.[1] T.R. Henn in The Lonely Tower finds six major phases in him, a division which can be reduced substantially on the principle of classification and exclusiveness.[2] Charles Williams in Poetry at Present finds two Mr. Yeats, the first Mr. Yeats of his early poems and the second Mr. Yeats of his later poems.[3] This is a kind of convenient tidying up, for there is not just a first and a second Yeats but a third one too as seen, for example, in his A Vision (1925; revised edition, 1937) with its 'quasi identity', its odd schemetizations, its pseudo-mathematics and its disjunctive mysticism. Notwithstanding this work, a unit by itself, Yeats's poetry is neither bipartite nor tripartite but one with continuity and growth.

Yeats has often been compared to Eliot. Both possessed a magnificant intelligence; both show a profound development. And yet there is a sharp difference between them and that in the nature of their experience and its expression. Eliot believed that disparate experiences like falling in love, reading Spinoza, hearing the noise of the typewriter or getting the smell of cooking egg, can be in the mind of poet amalgamated to form new wholes. This was the view of a metaphysical and absolutely—as far as that can be in poetry—of a detached and impersonal poet. Yeats was in contrast, a highly personal poet whose experience was free of trivia and bric-a-brac and who moved and climbed in seriousness pinnacles of poetic achievement through irony, hatred, violence, sex, religion, philosophy and art.

Yeats can be approached in many ways : the man and the mask as Richard Ellmann does in his two books, The Man the Masks (1949) and The Identity of Yeats (1954), the divided image as Margarat Rudd postulates in Divided Image (1953), the growth of his poems in Jon Stallworthy's Between the Lines (1963) or contrariness as B. Rajan explicates in his recent book W.B. Yeats : A Critical Introduction (1965). The thesis I should like to make out here is that Yeats can be evaluated from another standpoint namely partial and total experience. The criterion of the partial or total experience of an author in a creative work can be applied to poetry of a kind like that by Yeats who is primarily a personal poet.

All experience can be used partially in conscious deliberation or wholly in creative accomplishment by a poet. If the experience is partial or delimited the result is that poem after poem is similar. W.H. Auden to a large extent, Cecil Day Lewis and Louis MacNeice show this kind of stereotype and hence they do not show as Elizabeth Jennings writes in Poetry To-day (1961) any startling development.[4] A growing poet has now experiences, each different from another in sharp ways; the experiences are in a continual process of forming new wholes. The total experience at any one point of time can be poured into a poem making it a self-sufficient and viable unit of both consciousness and communication. There are poems of this type in Yeats' poems of total experience.

The early Yeats followed Spenser, Shelley, Morris his master and Arthur Symons. We find this in the volumes The Wanderings of Oisin (1887), Crossways (1889), The Rose (1893), The Wind Among the Reeds (1899), In the Seven Woods (1904) and The Shadowy Waters (1906), The poems in these volumes are examples of partial experience. The poet had a fixed and single-minded purpose as he wrote in *Autobiographies* : 'In my heart I thought that only beautiful things should be painted, and only ancient things and the stuff of dream were beautiful'. He planned a mystical order with elfin fancies and the legend and folklore of Celtic Ireland. He took for subjects in which romanticism inhered as in *The Falling of the Leaves, The Lake Isle of Innisfree, The Song of Wandering Aengus, Aedh wishes for the Cloths cf Heaven.* All these poems contain partial experience inasmuch as dream is their chief constituent.[4] The temperament of the poet at the time was due partly to the literary tradition he followed and partly to the big Estates in which he lived and moved and where one was inevitably led to a bookish existence. Yeats at this time could not help being a kind of 'Il Fenseroso platonist' writing incantatory lyrics and esoteric prose. The world of actuality was shut out and that for some twenty years, and, so long as this happened, Yeats suffered from schizophrenia.

There were events which took Yeats out of his romantic languor and attenuated experience. The political uprisings of the time and the bloodshed and executions of political leaders shocked the poet. He wrote poems of realism like *September, 1913, Easter 1916, Nineteen Hundred and Nineteen, In Memory of Major Robert Gregory, Meditations in Time of Civil War.* He remembers martyrs of the past like O'Leary Edward Fitzgerald, Robert Emmet and Wolf Tone and exiles who 'maddened every mother's son' (*September, 1913*). The poet withers into the truth : 'A terrible beauty is born' (*Easter 1916*). The poems deal with violence and evil foot. The utterances are not just rhetorical : they are ratiocinative too for on the occasion of the greatest passion the poet is critical.[5]

Yeats's new experience of violence was further accentuated by other sinister experiences. He went to the theatre as a dream panegyrist but ended up in disillusionment with the behaviour of the audience at the performance of Synge's *Playboy of the Western World.* Then there was the Maud Gonne chapter in his life. The poet was rejected recollected in *Adam's Curse.* Maud Gonne once pallas Athene had become another destructive *Helen of Troy*. She became a symbol of hatred, an emotion which was increasingly exercised by the poet to produce his 'Fleurs du Mal' as in *Ribh considers Christian Love Insufficient* where he states' 'I study hatred with great diligence'.

The accumulation of these diverse personal experiences did not keep the poet at the personal level alone. Were it so, Yeats would be just another existentialist. He moved from the personal to the impersonal—the subjective to the objective, the relative to the absolute, and it is in this resolution and transcentalism that Yeats is a great poet. His impassioned intellectualism made him differentiate the man from the mask, the poetic self from the true self or the Self and Anti-self seen in several poems. In *A Dialogue of Self and Soul*, he accepts life and at the same time reproaches it : 'That defiling and disfigured shape'—old age. But the total resolution is that life is important, even as the soul is in *Sailing to Byzantium* in the life-soul conflict with which he dealt.

Each of Yeats's major poems is the result of gatherings of experience transformed by thought into perceptions or concepts and absolutes. A practical criticism of each poem on the basis of the experiences it holds and their resolution into a new creation will bear testimony to Yeats's maturity in using total experience for the making of a poem. Even in the analysis of the total experience there can be possible alternative criterion for the evaluation. I submit two methods for the investigation and demonstrate them, one through *Among School Children*, and the other through *Byzantium*.

The total experience of poet is enshrined within the poem itself and can be adducad therefrom and not by any excursion into extra-literary fields or biography whieh may or may not help. If the poet at a particular point of time pours out all his critical principles and creative impulses at that time into the poem, then an instance of total experience has occurred. Even a single poem thus can hold total experience. Yeats achieved this in a few major poems: He accomplished it in that moving intellectual poem *Among School Children* (1926). Here he was concerned with the 'actualization' of images or concepts. Images according to Yeats are immortal and reach the heights of the Absolute; they escape the onslaughts of time and age which beset life. They have their 'own order of existence'. The abstraction of the image in *Among School Children* is given through a human story complete by itself. The poet walks through the class room of the school children, half-ironical to himself, 'A sixty-year-old-public man'. He recalls Maud Gonne who told him a tale of 'harsh reproof' when she was at school and so the image of the little girl is set against the real school children. The image dominates the human scene and the poet seeks to find one among the school children who resembles the image. The image takes form and shape 'She stands before me as a living child'. The image returns newly turned to the mind : 'Her present image floats into the mind'. Thoughts now arise of Plato, Aristotle and Pythagoras; but they are summarily dismissed as they suffered death and decay. But images are beyond death or doom. They are real like the mother's image of her child or Christ's image for a nun. Life is illusory; but images are not for they are 'Presences'. The poet now moves to the climax of his final utterance. Labour blossoms into images; the body and the soul are equal peers; there is perfect unity of being as he poem ends in ecstasy or a cnaticle of joy :

> 'O chestnut-tress, great-rooted blossomer,
> Are you the leaf, the blossom or the bole ?
> O body swayed to music, O brightening glance,
> How can we know the dancer from the dance ?'

Writing on the conclusion of *Among School Children*, John Wain finds it 'unaided speculation' which 'leads nowhere'.[6] He expected the poem to circle back on itself and the early personal situation.[7] At all events why this should be is unconvincing. Thomas Parkinson in his book *W.B. Yeats: the Later Poetry* (1964) comments on the brevity and the shortcoming of these last tines as the idea in them does not run through the whole poem :

> 'Even in so great a poem as 'Among School Children'... we can still ask why the moment of enraptured apprehension of reality should be so brief, whether it does genuinely transcend the limits so fully and even affectionately treated in the bulk of the poem. The poem flirts with the danger of casting doubts on its own resolutions'.[8]

If the poetic method is to find what is central to the poetry of Yeats namely 'Unity of Being'[9] and that throughout this poem as a single and only theme, then perhaps there may be some reason for misgiving or dissatisfaction like that of Parkinson. But when the poem is taken as a whole the conclusion is logical at the end of the ideas in the poem and the quest of the poet. In the last four lines of the poem, the thought and the utterance are complete. Image has fused with personality and there is the affirmation of the higher truth. The poet gets his richest fulfilment or the fulness of Being. The whole poem, in fact, has moved upwards in a cosmic spiral, from life or the real world, to the world of abstraction or the image, and thence to Reality. If this accomplished range and depth within the poem does not convey total experience, then what does ?

There is another method of gauging the total experience and that is through the cultural context and the poetic context in a poem. Murray Kreiger in *A Window to Criticism* (1964) writes perceptively of the two contexts :

> 'on the one hand the unique existential context of cultural forces and there is on the other hand the unique poetic context of the literary work; but most pragmatically, there is the relation between the two, the extent to which and ways in which the later may be said to reflect the former'.[10]

The cultural and poetic contexts are not to remain in isolation but there must be a Hegelian flow between them. This is achieved by Yeats in Byzantium (1930), the Hamlet of modern criticism, for it has given rise to multiple interpretations as has

Shakespeare's Prince of Denmark. The poem is an excellent one for the study of the image, the poet and the persons, tension, contrariness and stylistics in poetry. It can also be assessed at another level, the cultural context and the poetic context within the poem and the amount of experience it holds. An explication along these lines is worth a venture in criticism.

Byzantium was the capital of the Eastern Roman Empire or Eastern Christendom. It is identified with Constantinople now called Istanbul (Turkey). Yeats himself had written 'I think that in early Byzantium, may be never before or since on recorded history, religious, aesthetic and practical life are one'. (A Vision B). In 1908 Yeats saw gold and enamel works at Ravena; in 1925 he saw mosaics in Italy and Sicily. Byzantium becomes a symbol for the poet. It meant for him the perfect circle in the best Scholastic sense, a synthesis of the Hebraic, the Hellenic, the Gaelic Christian and the mathematical perfection of Byzantine artists. It was Yeats's New Jerusalem, his holy city, as Gogonooza was Blake's.

One aspect of the cultural context in Byzantium is the Eastern element which weaves in and out, first abdurately and next with a calmer insistence in spite of the entanglements in which all this is revealed. We are plunged into the city in its early history with its Sodom and Gomorah variant. There is 'The Emperor's drunken solidiery' (St. 1) referred to once before in the poem of Nineteen hundred and Nineteen. There are 'the night-walker's with their associations of sensuality (St. 1). There is 'The fury and the mire of human veins' (St. 1). This was Byzantium in violence and disarray before art and measurement brought order. The triumph of form came with 'the golden smithies' who wrought :

'Miracle, bird or golden handiwork,
More miracle than bird or handiwork,
Planted on the star-lit golden bough' (St. 3).

These gifted 'smithies break the flood' (St. 5) or the irrational. There is the exaltation of reason as the mosaic workers lay down the 'Marbles of the dancing floor' (St. 5) or achieve beatitude as dance symbolizes. Simultaneous with the Eastern or pagan thought is the Western or Christian thought in the cultural context of the poem. There is the Cathedral of St. Sophia, symbol of Christianity. There is the dome (St. 1) of the Church, the 'image of heaven, the only canopy for God'.[11] Then there is the great Cathedral gong whose resonance closes the poem (St. 5). The advanced Yeats of the later poems sought identities, the identity with Christianity, for instance, although he was not an orthodox Christian himself and did not subscribe to Christian dogmas as does T.S. Eliot. In fact, Yeats 'believed in nothing yet spoke for belief.'[12]

The cultural context in the poem thus has two themes, Eastern and Western, which comes through the poem. In addition, there is the poetic context or the original ideas of the poet on life and death, sex, and spiritual experience. There is a reference to 'death-in-lift and life-in-death' (St. 2). Further there is the exploration of death itself:

> 'For Hades' bobbin found in mummy-cloth
> May unwind the winding path' (St. 2).

The bobbin evokes the gyre symbol, a favourite mathematical term of the poet which helped him to explain the cycles of history or the cycle of life. The bobbin winds and unwinds the thread in the revolving gyre. The dead are invoked in order 'to discover their wisdom'.[13]

There are sex symbols 'the cocks of Hades crow' (St. 3) representing the 'dominant untiring male'. There is 'the moon embittered' (St. 3), the moon symbol of womanhood. The sea (St. 5) which classes the poem, has far-reaching emotive and symbolic associations with both life and sex. There are baser levels of existence 'The fury and mire of human vein's (St. 1) and what is later described as the 'complexities of mire or blood' (St. 3). From this extremity of debaseness the poet goes to the other end of nobility or spiritual existence. He writes of 'Flames that no faggot feeds' (St. 4), and of 'Flames begotten of flame' (St. 4). Fire or flame is a symbol of martyrdom and purification. The holocaust is followed by crowning glory or consummatumest :

> 'Dying into a dance,
> An agony of trance,
> An agony of flame that cannot singe a sleeve' (St. 4).

In A Vision B p. 231 : Yeats refers to a Japanese play where the priest tells the girl 'cease to believe in flames and they will end'. She does not do so and suffers 'the agony of trance' or martyrdom for it is the flames which purify her soul.

The historical and sociological facts of Byzantium form the cultural context; the personal conceptual values of the poet comprise the poetic context. Both of these are evident and traceable in the poem. When these are isolated they remain as disparate experiences. But they are not so in the poem. There is a constant flow between the two and even a commingling. There is the dalphin, the sea-beast, symbolic of love. The allusion is to Arion who was flung overboard by the seamen; he saved himself riding a dolphin—'Astraddle on the dolphin's mire and blood' (St. 5). In News from the Delphic Orecle in last poems there is a similar reference : 'Straddling each a dolphin's back'.

The poem moves on to its great finals 'That dolphin-torn, that gong-tormented sea' (St. 5). The sea is torn by two forces, love (the dolphin) and religion (the gong). In the Cathedral of St. Sophia, Eastern and Western thought are united as are religion and love. The cultural context and the poetic context which appear momentarily separate, then flow one into another to separate again, are finally merged into one rapturous whole. Such a poetic process and a complex of achievement can only be if the experience which the poet or the person behind the poem has is not partial but total. This is the 'kind of vision which satisfies the whole being' (Italics mine), as Yeats once wrote to his father.

The early poems with their partial experience and the later ones with their total experience are not unrelated. In actuality, the later poems complete what was begun in the early poems. This can be gauged by a study of the density of the symbols, as he passed from poem to poem or one early poem to a later one. Dance, for instance, was first a symbol of blessedness in Oisin and the early poems; then a movement of life in Nineteen Hundred and Nineteen; then self-renunciation in The Double Vision of Michael Robartes: a girl dancing between a Sphinx and a Buddha or between wisdom and love: then the sexual act or the symbol of the fusion of opposites in Crazy Jane Grown Old looks at the Dancers. The mere fact that the symbol of the dance is not typological or with a fixed meaning shows the interlinking of the early and later poetry and that through the measure of whether it is partial or growing or total.

REFERENCES

1. R.P. Blackmur, Language as Gesture (London, 1954), p. 122.
2. T.R. Henn, The Lonely Tower (London, 1950), p. 34.
3. Charles Williamas, Poetry at Present (London, 1929), p. 58.
4. F. R. Leavis, New Bearings in English Poetry (London, 1942). Chapter I is devoted to the consideration of dream as the essential characteristic of nineteenth century poetry.
5. Richard Ellmann, The Identity of Yeats (London, 1954) p. 144.
6. Ed. John Wain, *Interpretations*: Yeats 'Among School Children' by John Wain (London, 1955), p. 210.
7. *Ibid.*
8. Thomas Parkinson, W. B. Yeats: The Later Poetry (London, 1964), p. 51.
9. C. K. Stead, *The New Poetic* (London, 1964), p. 13.
10. Murray Kreiger, A Window to Criticism: Shakespeare's Sonnets and Modern Poetics (Princeton, 1964), pp. 205-206.
11. T. R. Henn, Op. cit., p. 217.
12. M. L. Rosenthal, The Modern Poets: A Critical Introduction (New York, 1965), p. 32.
13. T. R. Henn, Op. cit., p. 218.

25

Rhythm in T.S. Eliot

Poetry can be studied at different levels—its semantics, its organic structure, and the emotional flux and the rhythm of its language. While scholarship always helps critical evaluation as F.R. Leavis persistently insists when he advocates in a critic not only the function of sensibility but close and relevant thinking,[1] the primary response of poetry comes from the language of the poet. The reader's mode of apprehension in poetry comes from the tones and nuances of words and their emotional content. Poetry deals with gesture in language, that which moves words, and it is such words which move us. That is the truth of the thesis of R.P. Blackmur in his laboriously critical book *Language as Gesture* (1954). There is gesture in all fine arts—'A good spire', for example, writes Blackmur, 'is weightless, springing, an arrow aimed at the Almighty'[2]. It is language as gesture which gives meaning—rather meaningfulness—and even if the meaning is critically overlooked (as it sometimes happens) the evocative power of words and their rhythm bring about that 'excited sense of being which we find in poetry'[3]. The heightened sense which poetry gives us makes it possibls at times to read it for the sheer pleasure of its emotion. Eliot, for example, enjoyed French poetry much before he 'could have translated two verses of it correctly'[4]. The poetry is the thing and the poetic intensity experienced is the essence of poetry.

There is a visual fallacy which often occurs when one reads poetry silently. Silent reading is critically all right when one peruses partisan or Imagist poetry. But where poetry is composed under the major conditions of complete creativeness, namely the functioning of the conscious and the unconscious in the poet, reading poetry aloud is essential for a just response and a full experience identical to that of the poet, as far as that can be achieved. Communication, whatever be the theoretical considerations of it, does pass between the poet and reader and that through heightened language and rhythm.

All rhythm is in consonance with a certain emotional flux or tension of the poet. The rhythm may be flowing or abrupt and may seek to confine itself to certain fixed patterns. The early Romans fitted in their rhythm to the dactylic hexameter, as Pope and his school to the Heroic Couplet, and his French contemporaries to the Alexandrine. When T.S. Eliot first published his volume of poems, Prufrock and other Observations in 1917, readers and critics brought up in the standard tastes of the nineteenth century, felt uneasy at some of the new poetry which this volume contained. But then, they were written in the traditional and the dream-laden style of the nineteenth century. Eliot's *La Figlia che Piange* is full of familiar soft music and poetical words like these lines from the poem:

(Read softly *in slow tempo)*

'Weave, weave the sunlight in your hair—
Clasp your flowers to you with a pained surprise—
Fling them to the ground and turn
With a fugitive resentment in your eyes:
But weave, weave the sunlight in your hair.'

In the next volume of Poems of 1920 also, there were a few Poems written in recognizable forms or the tight quatrains of Gautier with their alternate rhymes as in this stanza from *Burbank with a Baedaker*:

(Rhyme emphasis)

'Defunctive music under sea
Passed seaward with the passing bell
Slowly: the God Hercules
Had left him, that had loved him well.'

The same choice of a quatrain and a regular movement, partly without rhyme, is found in the stanzas of *Sweeney Among the Nightingales*:

(Rhyme emphasis)

'The host with someone indistinct
Converses at the door apart,
The nightingales are singing near
The Convent of the Sacred *Heart*'.

These Poems are full of order, discipline and sweetness and move in the manner of nineteenth century poetry.

Keats, Tennyson and the early Yeats, like Catullus, Verlains and Leopardi, wrote verses which are harmonious and sweet. This cloud-cuckoo-land type of singing verse received its final rendering in the special poetry of the Symbolists. After that, romanticism had waned and poetic diction and verse had become outworn by excessive use. Something, at this critical juncture, had to be done to stem the decadence of poetry. New forms and diction had to evolve in conformity with the progressive and complex are of our century and the no less complex experience of self-conscious modern poets. In this reaction and revival, Eliot played his part. He felt that the only way to find out a new vocabulary and a new rhythm is by impersonality in poetry.[5] He asserted, along with C.S. Lewis,[6] that the poet's personality is never revealed in poetry. If that is true, then dramatic poetry is the best and the most objective poetry which can be written. And so Eliot took to the writing of dramatic poems. He created a middle-aged lover with a bald patch on his head and made him speak not in the beats of regular verse but in the variation and the flexibility of speech rhythm:

(In conversational tone) 'Let us go then, you and I,
When the evening is spread out against the sky
Like a patient etherised upon a table;
Lat us go, through certain half-deserted streets,
The muttering retreats
Of restless nights in one-night cheap hotels
And sawdust restaurants with oyster-shells:'
(The Love Song of Alfred)

In the *Poems* of 1920 he wrote of old men in their senility. He makss Gerontion speak of himself in his characteristic manner in varying run-on lines:

(Read with drawl) 'Hhere I me, an old man in a dry month,
Being read to by a boy, waiting for rain.
I was neither at the hot gates
Nor fought in the warm rain
Nor knee deep in the dalt margh, heaving a cutlass,
Bitten by flies, fought.
My house is a decayed house,
I have no ghosts,
An old man in a draughty house
Under a windy knob.
....
Think at last
We have not reached conclusion, when I
Stiffen in a rented house.'

Eliot creates 'Apeneck Sweeney' and in describing him uses current speech. A lady wearing a Spanish cape sits

(Speed variation) 'on Sweeney's knees
(Quick) Slips and pulls the table cloth
Overturns a coffee-cup,
Reorganised upon the floor
(Slow) She yawns and draws a stocking up'.

Sweeney, this squalid modern lover, is sick in soul and so he walks up to the window :

(Speed variation) 'The silent man in mocha brown
Sprawls at the window-sill and gapes;
(fast) The waiter brings in oranges
Bananas figs and hothouse grapes;
(slow) The silent vertebrate in brown
Contracts and concentrates, withdraws'.

These lines are an example of current speech transformed into poetry by subtle selection and rhythmic arrangement. In this sensitizing of current speech, Eliot is different from Ezra Pound who considers all current speech as poetry. Distinction in phrasing, as Eliot perceives, can never exist unless it is created by distinction of sensibility.

When Eliot was thirty-four years old in 1922, he composed his masterpice, *The Waste Land.* This magnificent poem, like the poems in the earlier volumes, deals with the theme of the soul, its degeneration, and its groping for salvation in a calamitous world. It is a mighty subject mightily written in a variety of tones and styles. There is lyrical sweetness in the opulence of Elizabethan poetry like this Elizabeth and Leicester passage:

'Elizabeth and Leicester
Beating oars
The stern was formed
A gilded shell
Red and gold
The brick swell
Rippled both shores
Southwest wind
Carried *down stream* (fall of voice)
The peal of bells'.

In the part, the Fire Sermon, written after the manner of St. Augustine and the Buddha, he used varied lines and no punctuation. He refers to Carthage, cauldron of unholy loves', and purification by fire, in powerful lines which sear into the memory:

(Read to indicate torture)	'To Carthage then I came Burning burning burning burning *O Lord* Thou Pluckest me out *O Lord* Thou pluckest burning'

Still more dramatic is the description of the decomposition of civilization in the part, What the Thunder said. Eliot presants doom and destruction to warn sinful men. He sees the solid cities of the world disintegrate. The verse moves dramatically in keeping with the terrible vision of the poet:

(In rising forte)	'What is the *city* over the mountains Cracks and reforms and *bursts* in the violet air *Falling* towers Gerusalem Athens Alexandria Vienna London Unreal.'

Such a mood and such a thought could never fit in the sing-song and the namby pamby verses of the nineteenth century, where sweetness is the only test of poetry.

There are other potent lines in the poem as the poet enters into new corners of experience and of the mind. He presents fear and thinks that through this negative emotion perhaps mankind may be redeemed :

(Deep voice and very slow)	'Only There is *shadow* under this *red rock*, (Come in under the *shadow* of this *red rock*), And I will show you *something* different from either Your *shadow* at morning striding behind you Or your *shadow* at evening rising to meet you; I will show you *fear* in a handful of *dust*.'

He creates a neurotic woman and the verse at once splits and rushes in paroxysms. The verse sharply changes from frenzy to sobriety as the hysterical woman gets the answer to her question from cold reality. Mark the excitement of the one who replies:

(in alto) 'My nerves as bad to-night. Yes, bad. Stay with me.
Speak to me. Why do you never speak. Speak.
What are you thinking of? What thinking? What?
I never know what you are thinking. Think.'
(in bass) I think we are in rats' alley
Where the dead men lost their bones.

Eliot believes in the recitative power of verse. He states that the auditory imagination must function in the creation of poetry. But it should in no way care only for sounds apart from meaning like the poetry of Swinburne. A true auditory imagination creates the tangible image through sound proccesses like these lines of Eliot from *The Waste Land*:

'If there were the *sound* of water only
Not the cicada
And dry grass singing
But *sound* of water over a rock
Where the hermit-thrush sings in the pine trees
Drip drop drip drop drop drop drop
But there is no water'.

In the *Four Quartets* Eliot seems to have reached the climax of his art. The poems reveal to man the way to salvation and consequently written in sober, meditative verses of varied length and accent. Consider the controlled power and resonance of these lines from *The Dry Salvages*:

(Read long drawn out)

'The sea howl
And the sea yelp, are different voices
Often together heard: the whine in the rigging
The menace and caress of wave that breaks on water
The distant rote in the granite teeth,
And the wailing warning, from the approaching headland
Are all sea voices'.

In *Little Gidding* Eliot gives us Sprung Rhythm or the prosody of stress like Hopkins in lines like these which describe the descent of the Holy Ghost in rather difficult lines :

(speed)

'Midwinter spring is its own season
Sempiternal though sodden towards sundown,
Suspended in time, between pole and tropic.'

In a volume of light verse, *Old Possum's Book of Practical Cats,* Eliot gives us witty and irresistible poetry. He creates the world of the cats. The poems give us new thrills of rhythm. In a funny poem, *Shimpleshanks: the Railway Cat,* he gives us the track beats of a moving train. Note the movement of the train from the word 'Skimble':

(Stac cats)

'There's a whisper down the line at 11.39
When the Night Mail's ready to depart,
Saying 'Skimble where is Skimble has he gone to hunt the thimble?
We must find him or the train can't start.'
All the guards and all the porters and the stationmaster's daughters
They are searching high and low,
Saying 'Skimble where is Skimble for unless he's very nimble
Then the Night Mail just can't go,'

This rhythm issues from the modern world of sound and is an example of machine rhythm.

In 1933, delivering a lecture at New Haven Connecticut, Eliot stated that he wanted 'To get beyond poetry, as Beethoven, in his later works, strove to get beyond music'. He meant that poetry should be poetical without any one recognizing that it is so. In other words, poetry should have perfect meaning in perfect rhythm. This is what he accomplished in lines like those from the Choruses of *The Rock*:

(Slowly) 'Much is your reading, but not the Word of God,
Much is your building, but not the House of God.
(With passion) O Weariness of men who turn from GOD
To the grandeur of your mind and the glory of your action,
To arts and inventions and daring enterprises,
Though you forget the way to the Temple,
There is *one* who remembers the way to your door:
Life you may evade, but *Death* you shall not.'

REFERENCES

1. The Common Pursuit by Fr. Leavis (1952) p. 9.
2. Language as Gesture by R. P. Blackmur (19.4) p. 6.
3. *Ibid.* p 4.
4. Selected Essays by T. S. Eliot (1932) p. 237, 'Dante: The Inferno's.
5. 'Tradition and Individual Talent', *Selected Essays* p. 8: Eliot distinquishes between 'the man who suffers and the mind which creates'.
6. C. S. Lewis supports impersonality in poetry; E. M. W. Tillyard personality in Poetry. Their points of view are found in different volumes of *Essays and Studies*, later published in *The Personal Heresy*, O. U. P.

26

The Waste Land and Anthropology

The isolation of a quality or a theme in a work of literature is a research possibility which, if pursued, with diligence can lead to discovery. Fred Mayne, for example, in *The Wit and Satire of Bernard Shaw* published in 1967 has isolated the exercise of wit and evaluated it as a functional element in Shaw's dramatic production. The result is the perception of an important element in the texture of Shaw's plays. So has John Loofbourow done in *Thackeray and the Form of Fiction* (1964) where he analyses the novels through the complex technique of language. Anthropology in *The Waste Land* can be treated in similar manner. One can do it in an attenuated form as Maud Bodkin has done with poetry in her book *The Archetypal Patterns in Poetry: Psychological Studies of Imagination*, first published in 1934 and reprinted in several editions even as late as 1955 in the Oxford Paperbacks. She studies poetry from the standpoint of 'response' emanating from the sub-conscious or the race or archetypal patterns within the reader. It is possible through this method to study *Orestes* with *Hamlet*, as Gilbert Murray has done, to show the "eternal durability" between primitive man and modern man.[1]

The evaluation of Eliot's *The Waste Land* and anthropology does not aim at the correlation of the subjective or the collective unconscious within one and the poem but an objective estimate of the rearches in anthropology for a reading of the poem in one particular aspect. It is true that the researches of anthropology are vast in details, terms and scope, with its own methodology, and what the poet states is succinct and in an imaginative reconstruct. The details of a science can help define the concepts and reveal the sources which adequately motivate the emotions displayed in a poem.

There are two anthropological works to which Eliot has referred in his Notes to the poem, Sir James Frazer's *The Golden Bough* and Miss Jessie Weston's *From Ritual to Romance.* The first was published in 1890 and the second in 1920. Frazer did the pioneering work and Miss Weston acknowledging her indebtedness to him went further a field in new areas of research on medieval literature. Miss Weston's book is moderate in size whereas Frazer's work is massive spread out in 73 large volumes and published by Macmillan & Co. in 1955, price £18.18S. The work is in IX parts and is a sequence of separate dissertations. Frazer has collected a vast amount of facts and tenable hypothesis which he colligates to rediscover the 'splendid vision of the antique world' and to reveal' the slow and toilsome ascent of humanity from savagery to civilization.'[2] *The Golden Bough* is not just anthropology; but literature for it only 'states' but 'expresses' in the distinction of the two terms made by I.A. Richards. Frazer writes with great literary beauty and feeling. To many, for example, the church bells of Rome cannot be heard on the shore of the Lake of Nemi for it requires an awareness of circular time to connect the past with the present. Frazer had this perception; he writes: 'By the lake of Nemi I love to hear, if it be only in imagination, the distant chiming of the bells of Rome, and I would fain believe that their airy music may ring in the ears of my readers after it has ceased to vibrate in my own.'[3] If we eliminate these intuitive flights, the work still possesses a sizeable quantity of valuable anthropological data.

The title 'The Golden Bough' has a symbolic and cosmic meaning. The plant is the mistletoe entwined round the bole of the oak tree sacred to a god. It has small yellow berries which shine in the light and appear golden. The mistletoe has no roots in the earth and it does not soar skywards. The plant was regarded as central to the mythic life of the ancients for the position between heaven and earth is the safest place to escape mortality.

The ancients feared mortality but they were paradoxically precipitated towards it. Frazer in *The Magic Art and the Evolution of Kings*, Volume I, narrates the gruesome practice of how the priest held office till he was slain and the slayer succeeded him.[4] Divine men were put to death; so were kings and gods. 'Man in fact', writes Frazer in Part III *The Dying God*, 'created gods in his own likeness and being himself mortal he naturally supposed his creatures to be in the same sad predicament.[5] Gods were buried: Apollo it was assumed was buried at Delphi and it became a place of pilgrimage. 'Pythagoras', writes Frazer, 'is said to have carved an inscription on his tomb, setting forth how the god had been killed by the python and buried under the tripod'.[6] The god Cronus was buried in Sicily, Hermes at Hermopolis, Aphrodite at Cyprus and Ares at Thrace.[7]

It is significant that Eliot is preoccupied with death in *The Waste Land* in the larger Christian sense as well as in this ancient magical view. He writes of 'The Burial of the Dead', Section I, and 'Death by Water', Section IV. The Hanged Man in the Madame Sosotris passage and the Tarot Card of "The Hanged Man" is a direct reference to the hanged god of Frazer. So is the line 'That corpse you planted last year in your garden' (I, 70), the identity of the pagan god recognized by F.R. Leavis in *New Bearings in English Poetry*.[8]

The death of the god was next connected with its opposite, the resurrection of the god. This is described in detail by Frazer in 'The Ritual of Osiris'. Herodotus has a detailed account of the ritualistic manner of this which is worth a reading:

> 'On the nineteenth day of the month the people went down to the sea, the priests carrying a shrine which contained a golden casket. Into this casket they poured

fresh waster, and thereupon the spectators raised a shout that Osiris was found. After that they took some vegetable mould, mois'ened it with water, mixed it with precious spices and incense, and moulded the paste into a small moon-shaped image, which was then robed and ornamented. Thus it appears that the purpose of the ceremonies described by Plutarch was to represent dramatically, first, the search for the dead body of Osiris, and second its joyful discovery, followed by the resurrection of the dead god who came to life again in the new image of vegetable mould and spices.'[9]

From death to resurrection of the god was an advance of thought connecting mortality with immortality. Frazer writes with reference to the Ritual of Osiris observed by the Egyptians: 'And from the death and resurrection of the great god the Egyptians drew not only their support and sustenance in this life, but also their hope of a life eternal beyond the grave'.[10] Eliot has this ancient empirically ascertained norm or the basic connexion between mortality and immortality. To subserve this view he contrives to describe futile death '*The* rattle of the bones, and chuckle spread from ear to ear' (III, 186) or the emptiness of the drowning of Phlebas the Phoenician (IV). *The* poet *alights upon the* thought of immortality as he warns humanity:

'Consider Phlebas,

Who was once handsome and tall as you' (IV, 321). Earlier in the poem he had given the significance of the larger aspect of immortality from Dante's vision in *Divinia Commedia* in the lines:

> 'I had not thought death had undone so maay Sighs,
> short and *infrequent, wer inhaled*' (*i, 64-5*).

The first line is from canto 3 and the second from canto 4 of Inferno describing Limbo and the inhabitants there.

In *The Dying God* volume Frazer connects the death and the resurrection of the god with the cycles of the seasons.

This was a kind of prehension of reality within the limited knowledge of the ancients. The Egyptians were an agricultural people dependent on the growth of the corn. The slain deity was Osiris. Frazer writes: 'If Osiris was in one of his aspects as a god of the corn, nothing could be more natural than that he should be mourned at midsummer. For by that time the harvest was past, the fields were bare, the river (the Nile) ran low, life seemed to be suspended, the corn-god was dead.'[11] Further, 'And from the death and resurrection of the great god the Egyptians drew not only their support or sustenance in this life, but also their hope of a life eternal beyond the grave'.[12]

In the contextual setting of *The Waste Land* there is the movement of the cycles of the seasons with their richly stored meaning. There is the season of barrenness, Winter,

> 'covering
> Earth in forgetful snow, feedir g
> A little life with dried tubers' (i, 115-7).

There is blight in the garden with 'the sudden Frost' (I, 75). There is the 'winter dawn' with its brown fog' (I, 61) and 'winter noon' (III, 208). Then there is 'Summer' which surprised (I, 8). The Tarot Cards have affiliations with fertility rituals. The card, 'The drowned Phoenician Sailor' is that of the fertility god, Adonis, whose image was thrown annually in the sea, as a symbol of the death of summer thrown at Alexandria and picked up at Byblos indicating the resurrection of the god. There are 'hyacinths' one of the flowers associated with the vision of the slain vegetation god.[13] There is spring with the traditional element of the revival of the vegetation god and the foison of the earth. There is reference to the corpse (the slain vegetation god):

> 'Had it begun to sprout? Self it bloom this year?' (I, 72-3). The spring too is conjured up in the swallow passage apart from its recondite meaning of the Procne-Tereus story. Eliot preserves the vegetation myth along with the seasons and the anthropological determinates. Wlil

We can bifurcate the anthropological thought patterns in *The Waste Land*: what is derived from Frazer and what from Miss Jessie Weston's *From Ritual to Romance.* Miss Weston's researches start with Frazer and J.E. Harrison's *Themis* and then covers medieval texts. The sub-title of Miss Weston's book explains her point of view:

> 'An account of the Holy Grail from ancient ritual to Christian symbol'. She turns in retrospective logic to Vegetation Cults but with a difference emphasizing life not death. She is concerned as she writes with 'Attis regarded in his deified creative 'Logos' aspect, not Attis the dead youth'.[14] She deals with 'the subsuming myth' of the Fisher King—his sterility and also that of the animals and the earth. She adverts to his eventual restoration. The loss of virility 'brings about a suspension of the reproductive processes of Nature'.[15] The Percival versions insist on this, 'the sickness and disability of the ruler of the land, the Fisher King'.[16] He is then healed and like Gawain he has freed the waters and restored the land (*Percival* Ed. Hucker, p. 466). In *Parcival* the stress is on the King and his suffering and his restoration. The earliest Grail story deals with the central figure who is dead and the task of the Quester to restore him to life.[17]

The Fisher King sterility and eventual restoration is inextricably bound up with Nature and 'the Divine principle of life and Fertility'.[18] In one of the Grail manuscripts, maidens are raped in violation of old mysteries and the land is cursed. In Eliot there is the analogue—

> 'The change of Philomel, by the barbarous king
> So rudely forced' (II, 99-100)

stemming from the Grail Manuscript as well as Ovid's *Metamorphoses*, VI, Philomela, cited by Eliot in his Notes.

Eliot at times uses Miss Weston's work in obverse irony. Miss Weston writes: 'the Adonis Cults is the enforced loss of hair by the women taking part in their rites'.[19] Hair is a fertility symbol and the sacrifice of hair was done to aid the fertility god. In *The Waste Land* there is the intricate analogy of

> 'Under the firelight, under the brush, her hair
> Spread out in fiery points
> Glowed into words, then would be savagely still'.
> (II, 107-10).

There was the footwashing of Anfortas, the Fisher King, which precedes his restoration and the removal of the curse from the land. This is given in mocking frivolity:

> 'O the moon shone bright on Mrs Porter
> And on her daughter
> They wash their feet in soda water'. (III, 199-201).

All these references, and others besides, from the anthropological works of Frazer and Miss Weston have to be considered in any assembly of *The Waste Land.* They come in as a reinforcement to the pattern of the poem and obliquely illuminate the major themes of life, death and salvation. Eliot himself in the Notes to the poem acknowledged his indebtedness to the two works and recommended their perusal. The massive reading that entails is worth a venture for it gives a settled assurance of an important aspect of the poem. It enables too an understanding of the syncretistic method employed by the poet and the shaping spirit of the imagination. It also makes feasible a line of research on the Frontiers of Poetry or the relations between limitation and achievement in poetry, same as what Una Ellis-Fermor had acconplished in her pioneering work, *The Frontiers of Drama* (1945).

REFERENCES

1. Maud Bodkin, *The Archetypal Patterns in Poetry*, Oxford Paperback (1965), p. 2.
2. Sir James Frazer, *The Golden Bough*, Preface to the Second Edition, p. XXVII.

3. *Ibid.*, p. XXV.
4. Sir James Frazer, *The Golden Bough*, The Magic Art and the Evolution of Kings (London, 1955), p. 9.
5. *Ibid.*, Part III, The Dying God, p. 3.
6. *Ibid.* p. 4.
7. *Ibid.*
8. F. R. Leavis, *New Bearings in English Poetry*, (London, 1942), p. 111.
9. *The Golden Bough* Volume II, St. Martin's Library (London, 1957), p. 493.
10. *Ibid.*, p. 496.
11. *Ibid.*, p. 487.
12. *Ibid.*, p. 496.
13. F. R. Leavis, Op. Cit., p. 109.
14. Miss Weston, *From Ritual to Romance*, A Doubleday Anchor Book (London, 1957, Edn.), p. 10.
15. *Ibid.*, p. 23.
16. *Ibid.*, p. 13.
17. *Ibid.*, p. 120.
18. *Ibid.*, p. 114.
19. *Ibid.*, p. 51.

27

F. R. Leavis : A More Eliotian Critic Than Eliot Himself

R.S. Crane, a New Critic, in his book Critics and Criticism (1963) writes that besides The Aristotelian method there are other methods in criticism like the linguistic, the historical and the philosophical. There is this "pluralism" or multiplicity of critical languages. Each critic follows his own way. Longinius, Coleridge, Arnold set out in new directions. Of the two major critics of the Twentieth century who have influenced both criticism and literature are T.S. Eliot and F. R. Leavis. The two critics followed divergent methods but there are points of contact between them. George Watson in *The Literary Critics* (1962) writes that Leavis is a "more Eliotian critic than Eliot himself". This calls for subtle discrimination between them.

F. R. Leavis in The Common Pursuit (1952) makes a several confessional statements of Eliot's influence on him. He writes that "one of the Essays which I most admire" is Eliot's *The Function of Criticism* written in 1923. It is from this essay that Leavis agreed that the critic's function is "The common pursuit of true judgment" and it is from this phrase that he titled his book in 1952. Eliot's critical impact on Leavis was made by the early critical essays in *The Sacred Wood*. Although

Leavis believed in the defence of values he believed placing poets in "a hierarchy of excellence" as Eliot does. Eliot's essay on *Dante* most influenced the poet; in fact it influenced him for "forty years" as he wrote in *The Kenyon Review* (1952). Leavis too has his standard of excellence in the line of Wit and The Metaphysicals and Pope.

The pursuit of true judgment as opposed to personal prejudices and cranks, and the placing of poets in an order of excellance are the two points where Leavis and Eliot meet. For the rest they are at divergence or in contrast. Leavis calls himself a "literary critic" in the essay "literature and society" in *The Common Pursuit.* Eliot is a doctrinal critic as he says in *After Strange Gods* (1934) where he advocates "tradition" and "orthodoxy". Leavis's criticism is based on texts. Eliot goes out to extra-literary fields or "explorable" areas for the poet has other interests besides poetry as he writes in "The Frontiers of Criticism" published in *On Poetry and Poets* (1957). Leavis in *Revaluation* deals with "The Present of Poetry" and "the past as to the present". Eliot with "Tradition" for no art is created "ex nihila".

Leavis's antipathies of Eliot grew with Time. In "Mr. Eliot and Milton" in *The Common Pursuit* he calls him "Pontifical". He does not quite appreciate Eliot's first essay on Milton and his recantation of Milton in the second. Eliot changes his views or modifies them at certain intervals. He has two essays on Milton and two on Shelley. Leavis finds that Eliot has scholarship but no "dritical sensibility" or the capacity to develop "responses" in close and relevant thinking. In *The Common Pursuit* he discards Eliot's view of Tradition which he describes as "incisively and provocatively formulated".

Apart from this controversy, F. R. Leavis is a critic, in his own right, and that to a major literary critic.